ASIA PACIFIC SECURITY OUTLOOK 2003

The cosponsors of this project wish to thank

Asia Pacific Agenda Project

ASIA PACIFIC
SECURITY OUTLOOK
2003

edited by
Charles E. Morrison

cosponsored by

 ASEAN Institutes for Strategic
and International Studies

 East-West
Center

 Japan Center for
International Exchange

A N   A P A P   P R O J E C T

Tokyo • Japan Center for International Exchange • *New York*

The surnames of the authors and other persons mentioned in this book are
positioned according to country practice.

Copyediting by Deborah Forbis and Pamela J. Noda.
Cover and typographic design by Becky Davis, EDS Inc., Editorial &
Design Services. Typesetting and production by EDS Inc.

Printed in Japan.
ISBN 4-88907-063-x

Distributed outside Japan by Brookings Institution Press (1775 Massachusetts
Avenue, N.W., Washington, D.C. 20036-2188 U.S.A.) and Kinokuniya
Company Ltd. (5-38-1 Sakuragaoka, Setagaya-ku, Tokyo 156-8691 Japan).

Japan Center for International Exchange
9-7 Minami Azabu 4-chome, Minato-ku, Tokyo 106-0047 Japan
URL: http://www.jcie.or.jp

Japan Center for International Exchange, Inc. (JCIE/USA)
274 Madison Avenue, Suite 1102, New York, N.Y. 10016 U.S.A.
URL: http://www.jcie.org

Contents

Foreword

The *Asia Pacific Security Outlook* (APSO) began with the 1997 *Outlook*, published by the East-West Center, and has continued in subsequent years as a joint product of the ASEAN Institutes for Strategic and International Studies (ISIS), the East-West Center, and the Japan Center for International Exchange (JCIE) as a product of the Asia Pacific Agenda Project (APAP). The sponsoring organizations are grateful for the continuing financial support of the APAP for the project and to JCIE for assuming responsibility for the workshop organization and the publication and distribution of the report. The APAP is designed to promote policy-oriented intellectual dialogue among nongovernmental analysts in the Asia Pacific region.

There are several regional security studies as well as global security reviews that include the region. We find these valuable, particularly the statistical information provided each year by the *Military Balance* of the International Institute for Strategic Studies in London.

This APSO survey is distinctive in several respects. First, the survey is the product of several institutions located in the region itself. It is not a view from the outside. Second, insofar as possible, the analysts come from the countries involved and present national perspectives. We make no attempt to provide a single authoritative view, although each year's overview weaves together some common elements and broad themes. Third, the survey process itself is intended as a "confidence-building measure," in which the analysts from the region exchange frank views with each other. In some respects, the published product is a by-product of the process rather than its end.

The APSO survey is intended to be analytical and descriptive, not quantitative or prescriptive. It deals primarily with attitudes and broad policy issues. It is intended to be forward-looking, covering developments of the previous year insofar as they have continuing relevance. The analysts come from nongovernmental institutions and, in some cases, from government-related institutions. They are asked to discuss governmental perspectives as well as influential views outside the

7

government. APSO covers only countries that are members of the ASEAN Regional Forum (ARF), but not necessarily all countries are covered every year. The editors take responsibility for the final product.

We are grateful to all those who contributed to the *Asia Pacific Security Outlook 2003*, most importantly the APSO analysts, who are listed at the back of the book. ISIS-Malaysia was the host institution for our November 2002 workshop, and we are grateful to Director General Dato' Mohamed Jawhar bin Hassan, who participated throughout the workshop, and his efficient staff, including Meilina Puteh. Wada Shū-ichi of JCIE coordinated administrative aspects of the project. Pamela J. Noda of JCIE oversaw the editorial process; she was assisted by Kawaguchi Chie. Deborah Forbis contributed to the copyediting. Others who assisted include Richard W. Baker, Patricia Matsunaga, and John Mercado of the East-West Center.

CHARLES E. MORRISON
PRESIDENT
EAST-WEST CENTER

JUSUF WANANDI
FOUNDING MEMBER
ASEAN INSTITUTES FOR
STRATEGIC AND INTERNATIONAL STUDIES

YAMAMOTO TADASHI
PRESIDENT
JAPAN CENTER FOR INTERNATIONAL EXCHANGE

Regional Overview

This is the seventh *Asia Pacific Security Outlook* since the annual report began in 1997. The 1997 report, prepared in late 1996, stated: "many agree that the regional security environment in the 1990s has been more benign than at any time in recent memory," and noted that none of the countries covered "is experiencing an acute security crisis nor is there a regional perception of a security crisis." Instead, the uncertainty was about the future environment, giving the region time to develop a climate of understanding and strengthen its new institutional machinery and confidence-building measures.

In retrospect, 1997 was an important turning point, and in 2003, the outlook looks much bleaker in many respects, but with some positive developments. The year is beginning with a serious crisis in the Korean peninsula and heightened terrorist concerns, especially in Southeast Asia. The prospect of an American-led military action to effect disarmament and "regime change" in Iraq is generally regarded with anxiety, by some because they fear a conflict will increase internal tensions and lead to more terrorism, and by others because they fear having to make politically difficult choices as to how far and in what way to support the American effort. Yet, larger power relationships in Asia Pacific are as healthy as they have ever been. The established states find common cause on many issues relating to terrorism; they cooperate at police and intelligence levels more effectively than before, and they are implementing with remarkable speed and unity new rules in areas as diverse as control of money laundering and enhancing cargo security.

Clearly, the Asian economic crisis, which began in mid-1997, played a critical role in creating the new and more sober political and economic assessment of the region following the hubris of the early and mid-1990s. Economic growth rates, then at the 6 percent–10 percent level in many developing Asian countries, have fallen to the 2 percent–4 percent range, with the exceptions of China, Vietnam, and South Korea. Unemployment is at historic highs in many of these same countries. Asia is faring better economically than other world regions, but it has never truly recovered from the 1997 economic crisis, and it is not meeting the high expectations generated in the 1980s and the first part of the 1990s.

Public confidence in government was also generally shaken by the 1997 economic crisis and similarly has never fully recovered. In the mid-1990s, with rare exceptions, state authority appeared to be consolidating, providing stronger internal order, and establishing solid units for international cooperation. In the two to three years after the onset of the economic crisis, many leaders were in political trouble, with the most dramatic casualty occurring in Indonesia where the fall of the long-ruling Suharto government took place in 1998. Indonesia remains in crisis.

The economic crisis also weakened the region's economic cooperation institutions, which were criticized for having failed to foresee or forestall the crisis or to react effectively once it had begun. The early and mid-1990s had witnessed a "bubble" of enthusiasm for regional organizations, with the Asia-Pacific Economic Cooperation (APEC) leaders meetings, the APEC Bogor vision, the APEC Osaka Action Agenda and Manila Action Plan, the Association of Southeast Asian Nation's (ASEAN's) expansion from six to ten members, and the establishment of the Asia-Europe Meeting (ASEM) all occurring in this period. No major regional institution collapsed, and there is a continuing creation of new processes, such as the ASEAN + 3 (China, Japan, and South Korea) group and the Shanghai Cooperation Organization (SCO), but the enthusiasm for regional economic cooperation has waned. In its place have come both restored interest in bilateral economic cooperation, including a plethora of free trade agreement proposals, and an emphasis on bilateral side-meetings and political statements in the framework of the larger multilateral meetings.

INTERNATIONAL TERRORISM

The past two years have witnessed the rise of terrorism to the highest place in Asia Pacific security concerns. Terrorism is certainly not new to the region, but in the past it was generally not regarded as transnational and was typically oriented toward local issues. Our 1997 *Asia Pacific Security Outlook* referred to the local conflicts in the Philippines, Chechnya, and Bougainville and also stated that the movements in these places "are or may be a terrorist threat far beyond their home areas." But it did not envision the international networks and training that we now know exist, and which existed even at that time in more nascent form.

A deepening concern with international terrorism has been the most dramatic change in the Asia Pacific security outlook since *Asia Pacific Security Outlook 2002*, along with the new Korean crisis. The region, like the world, was shocked by the scale and senselessness of the September 11, 2001, attacks in the United States, but at the time of our November 2001 workshop preparing the *Asia Pacific Security Outlook 2002*, the new "war on terrorism" was seen by the *Outlook* analysts, particularly those from Southeast Asia, as mainly an American war. Some analysts strongly believed that the terrorist threat was being exaggerated. But the intervening year has witnessed increasing evidence of international terrorist threats to Southeast Asian countries mainly coming from the Jemaah Islamiah (JI), a loose Islamic Southeast Asian network with ties to al Qaeda.

While evidence of the ambitions, connections, and potency of the JI was accumulating from arrests in Singapore and Malaysia as well as material found in Afghanistan, it was the killing of nearly 200 Indonesians, Australian, New Zealanders, Europeans, and others in the October 12, 2002, bombings in Bali that gave the threat high public awareness. For Southeast Asia and Oceania, the Bali bombings were almost as catalytic as September 11 had been for Americans and made it clear that terrorists would take advantage of vulnerabilities anywhere.

Northeast Asia remains something of an exception to heightened regional concern over international terrorism. China, Japan, and South Korea are all committed to fighting terrorism, and Japan and China have experienced terrorism on their own soil. The Japanese, however, do not look at Japan as a likely target of international terrorists, and terrorism in China has been largely confined to the far west, away from main population and economic centers. In South Korea and Japan, the successful holding of the World Cup games without a terrorist incident or even hooliganism strengthened local belief that terrorism was unlikely in these countries.

Outside the Asia Pacific area proper covered by this report, but involving member-countries of the ASEAN Regional Forum (ARF), other terrorist attacks have also deepened concern about terrorism. These include the attack on the Indian Parliament in late 2001 and the taking of hostages at a Moscow theater by Chechnyan terrorists, with the ultimate loss of 100 hostages and hostage takers. There is little doubt that terrorism will continue to be at the top of regional security concerns in the coming years.

THE NEW KOREA CRISIS

Perhaps the most surprising recent regional security development is the rapid onset of a full-blown crisis in the Korean peninsula. This was not foreseen by the *Outlook* team last year, although Korea certainly remained on its watch list. The demilitarized zone across the peninsula remains the world's most militarized boundary, but in recent years the opening of political dialogue between North and South Korea, particularly the June 2000 Korean summit, gave hope for improvement and some confidence in continued stability. After some loss of momentum, inter-Korean relations seemed to improve again in early 2002, accompanied by some quite dramatic economic policy experiments in the North. Even North Korean–U.S. relations, soured first by the Bush administration's relative indifference and then in January 2002 by the inclusion of the North in President George W. Bush's State of the Union address as a member of the "axis of evil," appeared to be starting a recovery when U.S. Secretary of State Colin Powell had an informal "chat" with North Korean Foreign Minister Paek Nam Sun at the July ARF meeting in Brunei, followed by the sending of U.S. Assistant Secretary of State James Kelly to Pyongyang in early October.

At the October meeting, the Americans confronted the North Koreans with evidence that they were engaged in a uranium enrichment program in violation of the 1994 Framework Agreement (under which the North Koreans had frozen their nuclear programs). Rather than denying this, according to American reports, the North Koreans admitted the program, with no apologies. After the North Korean admission became public knowledge, relations steadily worsened. U.S. shipments of fuel oil to North Korea under the 1994 agreement were cut off, and the Americans refused further discussions until North Korea abandoned its nuclear programs. The North Koreans pronounced the agreements dead and proceeded down a path similar to the one it had pursued almost a decade earlier. In almost staccato fashion, the North Koreans removed seals and surveillance equipment from their nuclear facilities, sent international inspectors packing, commenced moving fuel rods to their reactors, announced withdrawal from the

Nonproliferation Treaty (NPT), and suggested that they might resume missile tests. Asserting that its security was in danger, Pyongyang demanded a nonaggression treaty from the United States and other concessions. Washington reaffirmed that it would not negotiate under blackmail.

Although North Korea possibly has one or two nuclear weapons and certainly has the capability of producing several more in a relatively short time, the rest of the Asia Pacific region, including the United States, has generally downplayed the seriousness of the North Korean challenge, hoping that the issue can be resolved through diplomacy. But as the year 2003 opened, it was unclear that this avenue would work. Some believe that once the uranium enrichment program was exposed, the North Koreans had decided to provoke the crisis while the Americans were distracted by Iraq in order to acquire a few nuclear weapons. A larger group of analysts emphasize North Korea's interest in economic aid, direct dialogue, security assurances, and recognition. The powers around the North—Japan, China, Russia, and South Korea—are all united in opposing a North Korean nuclear capability, but are unenthusiastic about using sanctions to accomplish this.

North Korea is said to have the capability of producing as many as five nuclear devices within months from the spent fuel they already have and of being able to build many more should their reprocessing plants become fully operational again. This capability is widely seen as a threat to the nonproliferation regime and a potential catalyst for the increase and/or spread of nuclear weapons elsewhere in Northeast Asia. Possible sales of technology or devices to other government or groups by the penurious North Korean state is another deeply troubling concern. It seems very unlikely that other countries in the region will tolerate an operating plutonium factory in North Korea. This provides the hope that a critical mass of neighbors will pressure North Korea toward the diplomatic route, but it also suggests how serious the crisis will become if diplomacy fails.

Iraq and the United States

The possibility of an international conflict in the Persian Gulf is a major concern throughout the region, but most intensely in Muslim Southeast Asia. In much of Asia, the interest is less in the implications of the crisis for the broader international order as in the implications for the individual countries. At the November 2002 workshop, the *Outlook* team itself was close to evenly divided on the issue of whether military action against Iraq may be warranted if Iraq does not meet the expectations of the international inspection process. But all felt that possible U.S. military action against Iraq would have a negative impact on the overall Asia Pacific security outlook. Some, particularly in Muslim parts of Southeast Asia, believe that military action against Iraq could be very divisive or even destabilizing for their societies and would create more terrorism rather than help resolve the problem. Only four of the team felt their own countries should fully contribute to an international coalition, and for two members this support was conditional on clear UN authorization.

An underlying concern for many non-Americans in the case of both the North Korea and Iraq issues is that decisions affecting all countries' security are being made in Washington. The policy communities in other countries feel that they have little influence over these decisions and that their own interests may not be taken into account or even well known. Some of the *Outlook* team felt that the United States was making policy on the basis of a narrow set of domestic interests or prejudices, and thus that its actions do not have the legitimacy required to make them truly effective in the longer term. Others felt that the lack of action by other actors requires the United States to take leadership and set an agenda.

China's New Diplomacy

Each year *Outlook* analysts have consistently agreed with the proposition offered in our annual questionnaire that "how China emerges as a great power is the biggest uncertainty in the region." Of the 2003 *Outlook* analysts, 16 agreed with this statement, two were neutral, and none disagreed.

China has more neighbors than any other country in the world, and at one time or another during the past 50 years, it has been in conflict or confrontation with most of those neighbors. But in the early part of the 21st century, China enjoys positive relations with all the countries around it. The recent and general improvement in China's relations with its neighbors was a noticeable feature of the *Outlook* 2003 workshop.

Aside from individual country considerations, there seem several reasons for the unanimous positive attitudes toward China:

- Chinese diplomatic efforts to deepen economic and political co-operation with neighboring countries. China's 2001 free trade initiative with ASEAN, its joining ASEAN countries in a 2002 declaration on the South China Sea promising to take no provocative acts, and its leadership of the Central Asian countries in the Shanghai cooperation process all stand out as important developments in China's outreach to neighboring countries. Farther afield, China significantly improved its relations with the United States by supporting the war on terrorism and toning down opposition to the U.S. ballistic missile defense system. Relations with Russia continue to be good, while those with India have been steadily improving.
- China's growing economic relations with countries of the region. China's continuing economic growth while much of the region is in stagnation has been both a source of attraction for other Asia Pacific countries as well as a matter of concern in the region. China is increasing its economic importance throughout Asia as a manufacturing center, a market, and a source of investment funds. The growth of economic ties has given business people from around the region a great stake in positive relations between their countries and China.
- The less belligerent tone in China's relations with Taiwan. While accepting the one China policy, the Asia Pacific countries generally see China's attitude toward Taiwan as an indicator of how it might treat neighboring countries in the future. For this reason, the less threatening tone in Chinese rhetoric toward Taiwan and support for direct economic and communications links across the Taiwan Strait are positively regarded throughout the region. Still, the projection of China's relations with Taiwan and Tibet's Dalai Lama into foreign affairs continue to be an irritant with countries as widely spread in the region as Mongolia, Indonesia, and some of the Pacific island nations.

Looking back over the past quarter century, China's reemergence as a central power in Asia has been quite spectacular. In the early 1980s, Chinese cities were markedly different from those of most Asian countries and the world, communications were primitive, there was little understanding of international diplomacy or law, and Chinese seemed awkward and uncertain in many international gatherings. China is today an integral part of the region's economy, it is a member of all major regional organizations and the World Trade Organization, and it is gaining confidence in playing leadership roles.

OTHER WATCH LIST ISSUES

Among other issues on the APSO watch list, large power relations continue to be stable, or—in the view of the *Outlook* security analysts—neither significantly improving nor deteriorating. Despite the leadership changes in the United States two years ago and in China in 2002–2003, which some thought might cause new difficulties in Sino-U.S. relations and heighten differences over Taiwan, the relationship appears outwardly harmonious. In both countries, however, a significant body of opinion sees the other as a rival. Another problematic large power relationship, that between Japan and Russia, is also stable. The dispute over the Northern Territories seems as far from a solution as it has always been, but Japan and Russia are emphasizing other aspects in their relationship, with new gas pipelines an important prospect.

The *Outlook* 2003 analysts also saw no major changes in two other watch list issues—arms purchases and territorial disputes. These were seen as problematic issues in 1997–1998, but in line with the generally improved relations among the governments in the region, they are now less salient than they once were. With the partial exception of the Taiwan Strait, most arms purchases seem related to modernization and new functions, and they are not regarded as problematic in neighboring countries. (For an overview of defense spending in Asia Pacific and armed forces strength, see table 1.)

The many territorial disputes in the region were largely quiet in 2002, with Indonesia and Malaysia resolving an ownership question over two disputed islands through the international court. At the ASEAN leaders meeting in November, China and the ASEAN countries declared that they would not take actions disrupting the status quo in the South China Sea. It was not quite a "code of conduct," as desired by some ASEAN countries, but there has been a noticeable drop-off in incidents in this area. Demarcation of some land boundaries, such as that between China and Vietnam, is continuing. However, the lack of incidents in 2002 cannot be considered too comforting. Territorial conflicts can be highly volatile and can flare up almost momentarily.

A final watch list issue, Indonesia, remains a serious security concern with implications for the rest of the region. Although there are signs of improved political stability associated with the transfer of leadership in 2001 and a lessening of some separatist and sectarian conflicts, as pointed out in the Indonesia chapter in this volume, Indonesia continues to face very difficult and fundamental challenges.

Table 1. Asia Pacific Defense Spending and Armed Forces (2001)

Country	Defense Spending[a] US$ m.	% GDP	Rank	GDP US$ m.	Rank	Armed Forces[b] Number	Rank	% Pop.	Rank	Population in 1,000s	Rank
United States	329,071	3.2	9	10,200,000	1	1,414,000	3	0.49	12	285,900	4
Europe (EU/NATO)[c]	144,948	2.0	14	7,204,000	2	1,495,240	2	0.43	14	350,944	3
Japan	40,300	1.0	20	4,100,000	3	239,900	13	0.19	18	127,300	7
Russia	7,500	0.5	24	1,522,000	4	988,100	6	0.68	8	144,700	6
China[d]	47,000	3.9	6	1,200,000	5	2,270,000	1	0.18	19	1,293,239	1
Canada	7,900	1.1	19	700,000	6	52,300	18	0.17	20	31,000	13
India	14,300	2.9	10	490,000	7	1,298,000	4	0.13	23	1,025,100	2
South Korea	11,400	2.7	11	422,000	8	686,000	7	1.45	5	47,295	11
Australia	6,900	1.9	15	358,000	9	50,920	19	0.27	16	19,015	17
Taiwan	10,700	3.7	8	290,000	10	370,000	10	1.67	3	22,124	15
Indonesia	878	0.6	23	145,000	11	297,000	12	0.14	21	214,800	5
Thailand	1,900	1.7	16	112,000	12	306,000	11	0.50	11	61,586	10
Malaysia	3,300	3.8	7	87,000	13	100,000	16	0.45	13	22,092	16
Singapore	4,400	5.2	5	85,000	14	60,500	17	1.64	4	3,691	22
Philippines	1,100	1.5	17	72,000	15	106,000	15	0.14	22	77,100	9
New Zealand	677	1.4	18	47,500	16	8,710	22	0.23	17	3,800	21
Vietnam	2,400	7.3	2	33,000	18	484,000	8	0.60	9	80,976	8
North Korea	2,100	11.7	1	18,000	19	1,082,000	5	4.42	1	24,500	14
Brunei	285	5.5	4	5,200	20	7,000	23	2.10	2	334	24
Cambodia	192	5.8	3	3,300	21	125,000	14	1.09	6	11,450	18
Papua New Guinea	27	0.9	22	3,100	22	3,100	24	0.06	24	4,899	20
Mongolia	25	2.5	12	1,000	24	9,100	21	0.35	15	2,600	23

SOURCE: Based on data from The Military Balance 2002/2003. London: International Institute of Strategic Studies (IISS), 2002.

[a] Defense spending figures are IISS estimates of total defense spending (not official budgets).

[b] Figures are for active duty regular armed forces.

[c] Europe figures are for the 11 members of the European Union that are also members of the North Atlantic Treaty Organization: Belgium, Denmark, France, Germany, Greece, Italy, Luxembourg, the Netherlands, Portugal, Spain, and the United Kingdom.

[d] GDP and defense spending estimates for China are based on purchasing power parity, including extra-budgetary military spending (China's official 2001 defense budget was US$17 billion).

CONTRIBUTIONS TO REGIONAL
AND GLOBAL COMMUNITY

Among the brighter spots in the regional security outlook is the growing attention that Asia Pacific countries seem to be paying to regional and global security issues. Not many years ago, contributions to international peacekeeping were relatively rare in Asia and the Pacific. Today, as the country chapters in this volume indicate, most countries contribute in some fashion beyond maintaining domestic order, and some are prepared to further increase these contributions. Moreover, regional countries are increasingly accepting outside involvement by friendly countries in internal affairs as in the case of Indonesia's acceptance of outside monitors for the agreements it has reached with the Free Aceh Movement.

Moreover, the September 11, 2001, attacks in the United States and the October 12, 2002, Bali bombings have greatly strengthened international cooperation. In the period since September 11, intelligence and police cooperation has been reinforced, as illustrated quite dramatically in the international effort that went into helping the Indonesian police in their investigations in the Bali bombings. Similarly, there was significant South Korean–Japanese police cooperation to ensure a safe World Cup.

The year 2003 promises to be a significant one for the Asia Pacific security order. Both the Iraq and Korea crises are likely to come to a head in the early part of the year, while the war against international terrorism will be a continuing one. The basic interests of the established states in supporting each other and improved cooperation should help the region weather this difficult period. Spurred by the recent and ongoing challenges, there are definite signs of growing maturity and confidence in regional relationships and thus in the overall security outlook.

Still, as reflected in the *Outlook* analysts' discussions in 2002, the relationships, arrangements, and institutions that have been established over the past two decades remain young and relatively fragile. And as demonstrated by the rapidity of the new confrontation with Iraq and the crisis on the Korean peninsula, the times remain perilous, and volatile issues continue to threaten the security environment.

Thus as 2003 opens, it is impossible to predict whether 2003 is more likely to be a year of wise leadership, positive accomplishments, and progress or one of miscalculations, lost opportunities, and tragedy on the regional (and global) scene.

ASIA PACIFIC SECURITY OUTLOOK 2003

1 Australia

The Security Environment

The October 12, 2002, bombings in Bali brought international terrorism to Australia's doorstep and made counter-terrorism the country's priority defense and security issue. The bombings, in which 88 Australians lost their lives, resulted in the country's largest civilian death toll since World War II. Australians already had heightened security fears after the September 11, 2001, attacks in the United States. But those concerns increased greatly after Bali and became focused on the urgent need for strong measures against terrorism.

More Australians died in Bali than any other foreign nationals. Whether or not the Bali terrorists were specifically targeting Australians, there was a widespread belief in Australia that they were being targeted and could be targeted again, either where Australians go abroad or in Australia itself. Under pressure to address ongoing and new security needs in its own neighborhood, support anti-terrorist measures in Afghanistan, and address the issue of Iraq's defiance of UN Security Council resolutions on disarmament, Australia faces increased pressures on its established defense priorities, levels of resource provision, and security organization.

INTERNAL   According to the Australian Security Intelligence Organization (ASIO), there are in Australia members of al Qaeda, as well as some Australians, who have received advanced terrorist training in Pakistan and Afghanistan. Australia is taking steps to strengthen its domestic precautions against terrorism. Tough new laws have been enacted giving powers to proscribe terrorist organizations and providing heavy penalties for those found to be members of them. Having decided to double the anti-terrorist capability of its armed forces after September 11, the government further decided after the Bali bombings to strengthen its measures concerning immigration document fraud and visa security and to enhance the capabilities of the ASIO and the Australian Secret Intelligence Service (ASIS) to respond to terrorism. The government also wants to expand its sky-marshal program to include international flights and to enhance physical security at diplomatic missions overseas. There have been suggestions that a new ministry should be established to direct homeland security on a national scale.

EXTERNAL   The terrorist threat is global, but Australians see the Asia Pacific region as having special priority, not just because of the Bali incident, but also because concentrations of Australians are more likely to be found there and because of the ability of terrorists to exploit perceived weaknesses in other countries. It has become commonplace for Australians to acknowledge the volatility of their regional environment and the fragility of some of the states and state institutions in some countries. It is in this context that Prime Minister John Howard answered a journalist's question by saying that if a terrorist threat was not being addressed by a foreign country and that threat was directed against Australia, the government would, as a last resort, be prepared to take preemptive action. This comment triggered criticism in Southeast Asia.

Following September 11, a picture of terrorist networks in Southeast Asia has gradually emerged. Al Qaeda and other extremist networks within Asia were much more extensive and lethal than had previously been realized. Intended attacks on diplomatic missions of Australia, the United States, and the United Kingdom in Singapore in late 2001, foiled by Singaporean intelligence forces, illustrated the extent of planning and the broad reach of al Qaeda–linked operatives. It seems that the groups are diffuse and complex in their organization, well suited to operating in a globalized environment, and interlinked.

This web of organizations appears to have become entrenched in Southeast Asia, usually on the fringes of society. While some are focused on domestic opponents, others are prepared to target foreign interests and personnel, including Australians. It is also clear that some of these groups have links with terrorist and other extremist groups outside the region, particularly in the Middle East. The Australian government sees a need to meet this threat with a coordinated international response.

It looks to governments of individual countries as the principal partners for effective action against terrorism. It is seeking to develop a series of bilateral agreements with as many countries as possible. Indonesia is of particular importance. Australia is offering all possible assistance to the Indonesian authorities and looking for more effective ways to cooperate in the future. It has contributed up to 120 personnel to a joint operation against those responsible for the Bali bombings—an operation that has been marked by close cooperation and commendable progress.

Australians also vigorously support multilateral action, including through Asia-Pacific Economic Cooperation (APEC) meetings, as a means of providing support and encouragement for national governments. This new mindset is thus counteracting the tendency noted in earlier assessments in this series for Australia's policies on regional engagement to drift.

In the wider East and Northeast Asia region, where Australia's major economic interests are concentrated in its strong trade and investment relations with Japan, China, and South Korea, Australia continues to look to the United States to ensure that there are no adverse shifts in the balance among major powers, and to support peace.

DEFENSE POLICIES AND ISSUES

DEFENSE POLICY   The fundamental outlines of defense policy remain those set out in the white paper published in 2000. Australia assigns first priority to ensuring its own national defense and that of its direct approaches. Its other objectives, according to the white paper, include fostering the "stability, integrity and cohesion in its immediate neighborhood, working with the nations in Southeast Asia to maintain stability and cooperation, supporting strategic stability in the wider Asia Pacific region, and supporting the efforts of the international community in global security." From these priorities it derives strategic tasks, which include being capable of defending Australian territory from any credible attack, without relying on help from the combat forces of any other country. These priorities also require Australia to have sufficient forces to make a major contribution to the security of its immediate neighborhood. Other tasks include contributing to international coalitions to meet crises beyond its immediate neighborhood where Australian interests are engaged. Forces provided for coalition operations in support of wider interests are drawn from the base that is maintained for the defense of Australia and for operations in Australia's immediate region.

Force structure is designed to control the sea and air approaches to Australia and to be able to defeat incursions into its territory, as well as to contribute to the security of Australia's neighborhood and to supporting wider interests. The navy maintains major combat elements, including a surface force of six guided-missile frigates; three Anzac frigates (increasing to eight), together with onboard helicopters, supported by a replenishment ship and an oiler supply ship; and five (increasing to six) Collins-class submarines. The army maintains six high-readiness army battalions supported by a range of fire support, logistics, and transport assets; a number of lower-readiness units able to provide personnel for sustainment and rotation; and a reserve force designed to sustain, reinforce, and rotate personnel, equipment, and Special Forces. The air force maintains a fighter force of three F/A 18 squadrons, supported by training squadrons, airborne early warning and control aircraft, air-to-air refueling aircraft, a wide-area surveillance system monitoring the northern approaches, and a range of ground radios and other support elements; a strike force of two F111 squadrons; and a maritime patrol force of two P3C squadrons.

Interoperability with the U.S. navy remains the principal focus for the Australian navy. The two governments have specifically agreed to promote interoperability between their submarine forces and to grant Australian access to U.S. research findings, analysis, and technology.

Personnel shortages are evident in several areas. Addressing a marked shortage in personnel is the most significant task facing the navy. No rapid improvement can be expected. Planned mitigating measures include increased use of the reserves and substitution of civilian for uniformed personnel. The air force also has personnel shortfalls in a number of key areas and is identifying opportunities for reducing activity in these areas.

The army is tasked to be able to sustain a brigade deployed on operations for extended periods and, at the same time, to maintain at least a battalion group available for deployment elsewhere. The 2000 white paper called for the army to reduce the number of brigades in its structure, without creating the substantial deficiencies in unit strength that had been normal, as well as to maintain high readiness levels. In order to achieve these objectives it will be necessary to draw on the reserves to directly provide fully trained personnel to frontline forces deployed on operations.

Deployments made in support of the U.S.-led campaign against terrorism (the additional costs for which are estimated at A$500 million [US$280 million at A$1.00 = US$0.56] for each period of three months), are stretching Australia's limited defense resources, and will distort the implementation of the white paper program unless substantial additional funding is provided. Australian political leadership has staunchly defended its commitments in Afghanistan, however, arguing that they are deployed in Australia's own interest, and are not there simply to support the United States.

Accumulating pressures are sharpening the choices that Australia has to make within current resource ceilings. On the one hand, advocates of more capable ground forces have taken the opportunity of U.S. pressures on Iraq, and the Australian government's desire to contribute to any needed offensive, to argue that the war on terrorism is global in scope and that regional needs should no longer be accorded a key place in determining Australia's defense force structure. On the other hand, it is argued that the region's security problems are Australia's problems and that Bali has sharpened the priority for Australia to attend to needs in its own region. Terrorism is a transnational problem, but it should not lead Australia to discard its regional focus in favor of a commitment to expeditionary capabilities designed for contribution to future U.S.-led coalitions farther afield. Australian defense policy is changing under the pressure of terrorist threats. Other changes can be expected in the balance between military and nonmilitary measures (such as intelligence gathering, protective security, and controls on the movement of people and money).

DEFENSE BUDGET   Total defense funding, on an accrual basis, in 2002–2003 is A$19.356 billion (US$10.839 billion). This amounts to 1.9 percent of gross domestic product. This incorporates the 3 percent increase in funding promised in the government's defense white paper of 2000. It also includes A$393 million (US$220 million) for operations in Afghanistan, border protection, and domestic security. Defense spending is expected to rise by 3 percent in real terms each year until 2010–2011. It will thus be A$20.7 billion (US$11.59 billion) in 2003–2004 and A$21.00 billion (US$11.76 billion) in 2004–2005.

Some A$3.239 billion (US$1.81 billion) will be provided for ongoing capital projects, and commitments have been made to new capital projects of A$6.4 billion (US$3.58 billion) planned to start in 2002–2003. Of this A$350 million (US$196 million) will be spent in the 2002–2003 fiscal year. Major new capital projects to commence in 2002–2003 include:

- Air-to-air refueling aircraft (5), capable of air-to-air refueling of fighter, strike, and surveillance aircraft;
- Direct-fire weapons (guided missiles) to equip the army's full-time infantry battalions and cavalry regiments as well as units that provide rotation and reinforcements to them;
- Additional (12) Trooplift helicopters to enhance capability to operate from troop-carrying ships;
- Battle-space communications for the army to provide modern deployable, networked communications infrastructure in the field;
- Electronic Warfare Self Protection (EWSP) for tactical aircraft against surface-to-air missiles for C-130 transport, and Chinook, Blackhawk, and Sea King helicopters;
- Aerospace combat and strike-capability options for replacing the F111 and F/A 18 fleets;
- Standard missiles for the FFGs;
- ANZAC Anti-Ship Missile Defense (ASMD) upgrades to combat systems and sensors;
- Air warfare destroyers—options for future maritime air warfare capability;
- Patrol boat replacements; and
- Armored personnel carriers upgrade.

Additional funding for operations to support Australia's contribution to the international coalition against terrorism amounts to A$194 million (US$108.64 million) (in addition to the A$330 million [US$184.8 million] provided in 2001–2002). This covers the deployment of Special Forces to Afghanistan and maintenance of a Navy Task Group in the Multinational Interception Force in the Persian Gulf and two Air Force 707 refuelers in the Kyrgyz Republic. Other additional operations to deter unauthorized boat arrivals and strengthen border protection received an additional A$22.3 million (US$12.49 million) in 2002–2003. Some A$219 million (US$122.64 million) has also been committed over four years to enable a doubling of the domestic counter-terrorist force.

Following the Bali incident, it is clear that increases in spending are needed to improve Australia's ability to protect itself against terrorism.

Both the prime minister and Defense Minister Robert Hill have foreshadowed these. Reviews have been commissioned.

CONTRIBUTIONS TO REGIONAL AND GLOBAL SECURITY

The Australian commitment to Afghanistan was substantial. It included four fighter aircraft, two maritime patrol and two refueling aircraft, Special Forces troops (150), three frigates, and one amphibious command ship—a total of some 1,500 personnel. This contribution was in support of the first invocation in 50 years of Australia's alliance treaty with the United States. Australia has also committed to Afghanistan some A$41.3 million (US$23.19 million) in humanitarian and reconstruction assistance, of which A$13 million (US$7.28 million) was delivered in 2002.

Before Bali, Australian attention had been moving to Iraq and the question of whether Australian readiness to support any U.S. attack on that country should be conditional on the attack being under UN auspices, as the country's participation in the 1990–1991 Gulf War had been. The government has firmly backed the U.S. and U.K. positions on Iraq and kept open the possibility of participating in an attack on Iraq even if the United States acted without UN endorsement or the support of most of its allies. Public opinion is divided, and only a minority would support military action not under UN auspices. A commitment of this kind would also put pressure on available defense resources. This issue has led to high-level questioning of defense priorities and policies.

Australia has taken a prominent role, intensified after Bali, in regional efforts to combat terrorism. It is in active liaison with relevant authorities of all regional countries. Memorandums of understanding on countering international terrorism have been signed with Indonesia, Malaysia, and Thailand, providing, among other things, for the exchange of information between law enforcement agencies and intelligence agencies. Similar bilateral agreements are being negotiated with other regional countries. It was under such an agreement that Australia and Indonesia set up the joint task force to pursue perpetrators of the Bali attacks, and Australia has offered Indonesia every support in that task.

Even after East Timor's independence in May 2002, Australia continues to provide a substantial force in that country, about 1,250 personnel mainly to secure the sensitive border with Indonesia. Australia is engaged in a gradual drawing down of this force. The cost of this presence and of the generation of additional forces to sustain it is estimated to be A$600 million (US$336 million) in 2002–2003 and A$563 million (US$315.28 million) in 2003–2004.

East Timor is training its own fledgling defense force and civilian police. Internal security remains a significant concern, underscored by riots in Dili toward the end of 2002. There are still large numbers of East Timorese refugees in Indonesian West Timor, including former militia members involved in the wholesale violence of 1999. In addition, problems of unemployment and of inadequate social and economic infrastructure will fuel continuing internal security problems, and require ongoing international assistance. There is a particular need to develop East Timor's court system to support the rule of law. For the post-UN period, Australia is seeking the development of an overall plan for international assistance to East Timor. Australia is continuing to deliver on its 2000 commitment of A$150 million (US$84 million) in development assistance over four years, with A$36 million (US$20.16 million) to be spent in 2002–2003. The objectives of the program are to assist in the development of a simple, effective, and sustainable government and administrative structure for East Timor, to support the process of reconciliation and peace building and the restoration of basic services, as well as to strengthen the productive sectors of the economy.

Australia also contributes significantly to stability in Papua New Guinea (PNG). Some A$343 million (US$192.08 million) in development assistance is directed toward strengthening governance, improving social indicators in health and education, building prospects for sustainable economic growth, and consolidating the peace process on Bougainville. Australia also provides some A$14.8 million (US$8.29 million) specifically for security, mainly in support of PNG government initiatives to reform and downsize the PNG Defense Force. Some 190 Australian military personnel support the peace process in Bougainville, although some reductions are being planned. An agreement between Bougainville and the PNG national authorities has been reached under which there is to be a referendum in 10 to 15 years on Bougainville's future status. In the interim, Bougainville is to enjoy a high degree of autonomy with its own police, public service, and judiciary and will be able to plan its own economic development.

Elsewhere in the South Pacific, Australian development assistance totalling A$165 million (US$92.4 million) seeks to assist the small island states to achieve the maximum self-reliance, focusing particularly on improving governance. In the Solomon Islands, where the negotiated resolution to recent ethnic conflict still requires external support, Australia provides ongoing assistance in the form of a major naval vessel and associated support personnel.

2 Brunei Darussalam

THE SECURITY ENVIRONMENT

The people and government of Brunei Darussalam take pride in a stable and peaceful state with an established ruling sultanate. No Brunei resident has been the victim or perpetrator of any terrorist activity, and the country was only marginally affected by the consequences of the September 11, 2001, terrorist attacks in the United States. Nevertheless, as a very small country bifurcated by Malaysia's Sarawak, with a wealthy and highly mobile population, there is strong awareness of Brunei's vulnerability to the outside and increasing anxiety about the stability of the Southeast Asian and larger global environment.

Brunei felt relieved in staging a successful Association of Southeast Asian Nations (ASEAN) Foreign Ministers Meeting in July 2002, followed by an equally satisfactory meeting of the ASEAN Regional Forum (ARF). Aside from the extra care to security required to host such meetings, the subject of terrorism dominated the meetings, reminding Bruneians of the priority their ASEAN partners and others place on the topic. The ASEAN ministers signed a pact with their most important dialogue partner, the United States, on counter-terrorism measures. Three months later, the sense of security was shaken again in an even more visible way by the October 12 bombings in Bali, a popular destination to which Brunei's national carrier has regular flights.

The message for Bruneians was that extremists and religious zealots can be active anywhere, a fact underscored after Bali when Australia, the United Kingdom, and the United States included Brunei on travel alerts advising their citizens to avoid or take extra caution in visiting Muslim areas of Southeast Asia. The reaction in Brunei was one of disbelief and dismay that their peaceful nation would be subject to such unjustifiable action. Nonetheless, information from arrested al Qaeda and Jemaah Islamiah (JI) members brought to light plans of the militants to create chaos in the short term with long-term intentions of establishing a Pan-Islamic state comprising Singapore, Malaysia, Indonesia, Mindanao, and Brunei. Thus, Brunei's fears are not just of violence and destruction to life and property, but also of a larger threat to the very survival of the state and its political system.

Transnational political terrorism is the main cause of current insecurities. A threat could be transmitted from the outside through deviationist teachings that might question the nature of the political system and the entrenched social hierarchies. Therefore, Brunei does not compromise on any deviation from its prescribed Islamic faith, taking tough measures against individuals or groups who espouse a different version. The government continually reinforces the state ideology of Melayu-Islam-Beraja (MIB), or Malay-Islamic-Monarchy. So far there is no indication of local support for JI or the Pan-Islamic proposal.

Aside from outside terrorists, nontraditional threats of growing concern include smuggling, drug trafficking, illegal immigration, and crime. The smuggling of prohibited goods, counterfeiting of currency, house break-ins, and car thefts all seem to be increasing.

A final cause for concern has been the stagnant economy. While Brunei is wealthy by regional standards, with a per capita income of about US$14,000, there has been no growth or diversification away from dependence on oil and gas. Youth unemployment is growing. Brunei hopes to establish itself as a financial services center and as a hub for regional trade and tourism, but a recent UN Conference on Trade and Development (UNCTAD) survey ranking it 128th of 140 states in its attractiveness for foreign investment gave no cause for comfort.

In response to the growing sense of unease, Brunei has intensified protection for infrastructure and its economic lifeline—oil and gas production and transportation facilities. It is also increasing patrols along its coast and inland waterways. And it has taken several steps, either on its own or with neighbors, to address the nontraditional security agenda.

DEFENSE POLICIES AND ISSUES

Defense is a well-guarded policy area, hardly the subject of public debate or even interest. In 2001, there had been some indication that

Brunei might publish a defense white paper, probably using the Australian model. If there was one, it was not made public. Nevertheless, the mission of the armed forces is clearly articulated: to deter external aggression, terrorism, and any form of internal insurgency or public disorder. The mission also includes the goal of establishing good community relations. As for defense expenditures or budget allocations, no details are published, except what is available in the Eighth National Development Plan 2001–2005 introduced in 2000.

No major increase in the force size or shift in the defense policy is envisaged for the coming years. The land forces continue to operate with three regular battalions plus a support battalion. The air force is expanding gradually to increase its air defense capability as well as providing logistic support for other units of the armed forces. It is, however, in its infancy, with personnel still undergoing training. One of the main functions is surveillance and protection of Brunei's vast oil fields extending into the South China Sea and at the edge of the hotly contested Spratly Islands. The air force's parachute squadron has been more visible with frequent demonstrations during public parades. The air force is definitely more sophisticated now than when it began as the flying doctor service and then operated as an air wing of the armed forces until 1991, when the armed forces were restructured into today's units comprising land, air, naval, and service forces. The navy is equipped with assault boats and surface-to-surface missiles. Three navy vessels were ordered from the United Kingdom in 1998 for an estimated B$1 billion (US$580 million at B$1 = US$0.58). The first of the vessels built at the Glasgow shipyard was launched for sea trials in the United Kingdom in early 2002; it is fully equipped and capable of carrying a crew of 100. After sufficient training stints for its crew, it will join the other patrol vessels in Brunei waters.

The objective is not just modernization but also a strengthening of qualitative force, because the Brunei defense force represents one of the smallest and least equipped in comparison to those of Brunei's partners in ASEAN. Brunei has only about 5,000 armed services personnel, but Brunei's defense expenditures are greater than this number would suggest. Its suppliers include the United States, France, and Germany. In the fiscal year that ended March 2002, Brunei, with a bill of B$1.5 billion (US$870 million), was the second-largest purchaser of British-made arms outside the Middle East and had spent almost five times more than Malaysia's expenditure on arms from the United Kingdom for the same period. In seeking other hardware, Brunei has shown interest in buying Malaysian-built light aircraft that its air force is currently using. The vision of the Royal Brunei Armed Forces for the 21st century is to work "toward the effectiveness of the nation's defense." With that strategy in mind, the government is transforming the image of its defense forces. They are emerging as a professional force manned by well-educated personnel, not a force of school dropouts, as was their former reputation. More university graduates are joining the officer corps, indicating that the armed forces now enjoy a more favorable public image.

This new image is being cultivated through public and community relations activities. In addition to the usual parades by the armed forces on special occasions, the 41st anniversary of its formation was show-cased with a massive exhibition at the main shopping mall in downtown Bandar Seri Begawan. There was an array of vehicles, tanks, air defense systems such as the Rapier, short-and-long-range missiles, guns, artillery, and the like, while navy ships moored in the waters in the nearby Kampong Ayer were open for visits. Even the forces band was there to entertain the crowds while the medics offered free health services. The fact that the popular monarch is the defense minister, a post he has held since 1986, also boosts the public image of the armed forces.

Training is conducted locally and overseas. The most frequent exercises are by the land forces and the navy, in Brunei or elsewhere. The U.S. Navy and Marine Corps, comprising about 1,400 men, carried out a joint exercise with its Brunei counterparts in the second of a series of exercises. Naval exercises are also in force with Singapore and Indonesia, among others. Friendly naval visits are also common, especially from the Asia Pacific region, including from Japan and South Korea. Land forces hold regular exercises with forces from Australia and Singapore. Brunei possesses good jungle training facilities at Temburong, and this attracts foreign forces for joint training.

The government is activating several special task forces to deal with nonmilitary threats. In addition to the Royal Brunei Police Force, the Fire and Rescue Services, and the Gurkha Reserve Unit (strictly for guard and security services), other uniformed services are gaining prominence: the customs, immigration, labor, land, and transport departments and the Anti Narcotics Bureau. Together with the police, the concerned departments regularly mount checks and raids to weed out from society undesirable elements, be they illegal immigrants, drug traf-fickers, or illegal loggers and fishermen. This has prompted the government to expand the enforcement role of the agencies concerned. The religious authorities are also empowered to carry out their role as guardians of the faith against those who stray or break Islamic laws. National leaders are gradually viewing security issues in a comprehensive manner, and thus willing to mete out the burden of securing the environment to a larger segment of the population. Even the village head and civic leaders are expected to be on alert for any signs of disturbance.

Cooperation among several components of security providers appears to be an increasing trend. It is probable that civilians will be included in future exercises, as in the anti-terrorist drills at the international airport.

CONTRIBUTIONS TO REGIONAL AND GLOBAL SECURITY

As is often stressed by the head of state and government, Sultan Haji Hassanal Bolkiah, Brunei values its partnerships with its allies and neighbors. For a very small state, effective diplomacy and international goodwill and friendship can provide more safety and security than any amount of sophisticated weaponry. In that light, while not being complacent about military needs, Brunei places premium value on collective security and regional cooperation. Both the sultan and the foreign minister speak regularly against global terrorism at international and regional meetings. ASEAN is Brunei's foundation for exercising its sovereignty and confidence in external relations. For religious and culturally shared beliefs it considers the Organization of the Islamic Conference (OIC) of great significance, just as it attaches weight to the Asia-Pacific Economic Cooperation (APEC) forum to provide broader Asia Pacific relationships and economic cooperation. The most important global role it sees for itself is through the United Nations. Brunei attaches great belief in the universal values of the United Nations and its defense of threatened small states.

Brunei continues to host major meetings of ASEAN and other international groups without any problems. Therefore, it enjoys a good reputation as a safe and quiet place for conventions, away from the distractions and security scares of larger centers. It is committed to taking the necessary security measures to ensure that this reputation and source of income continue.

Brunei actively promotes intelligence sharing with friendly nations through a network of contacts. In this respect its regular high-level meetings with Malaysia under the Defense Cooperation Committee are important for both military and nonmilitary security matters. Search and rescue exercises with Malaysia are also invaluable as the two countries share sea and land borders. The outstanding border issues are regularly discussed at the joint commission meetings held in alternate venues. Brunei has agreed to establish consulates in Kuching and Kota Kinabalu to serve the increased social and economic links with the neighboring Malaysian states of Sarawak and Sabah. The political and military ties with Singapore are also strong, and the Singaporean use of the jungle training camp in Temburong continues to cement that close relationship.

The visits of Japanese coast guard ships and the proposals for patrolling the busy sea lanes against piracy would be an area of bilateral cooperation with regional implications. With the realization of the ASEAN +3 (China, Japan, and South Korea) regional community, there will be even closer cooperation with the armed forces of these Northeast Asian countries. China has expressed its interest in developing military ties with Brunei. The contribution of the ASEAN +3 countries may be most likely in the naval areas of cooperation. Concerning bilateral cooperation from outside the region, the continued close cooperation of the United Kingdom's defense establishment with the Brunei armed forces, in training, procurement, and general military cooperation and with the presence of the British Garrison (the Gurka Battalion) in Seria, offers a sense of security.

Frequent exchange of visits among political and military leaders is a sign of the interdependent nature of the security environment. The sultan takes a personal interest in military matters, as was evident during his three-day official visit to Thailand where military-related programs were on his itinerary. In December 2002, the sultan visited the United States and held talks with President George W. Bush, Secretary of State Colin Powell, and other officials. He also visited Fort Bragg military base and West Point military academy, strengthening the close military cooperation between the United States and Brunei. In January 2003, the sultan, during a meeting with British Prime Minister Tony Blair, signed an agreement for the continued stationing of a battalion of the British Brigade of Gurkhas in Brunei for an additional five years.

In Brunei, security-related matters are highly concentrated within the governmental structure, and the concept of track two discussions has not been fully explored. There is no autonomous think tank as in other ASEAN states for the exchange of information and personnel or for organizing security-related forums. The sole organization, the

National Institute for Policy and Strategic Studies, a member of the ASEAN Institutes for International and Strategic Studies (ASEAN-ISIS) and the Council for Security Cooperation in Asia Pacific (CSCAP), is located within the Ministry of Foreign Affairs. Occasionally the institute has asked academics from the university to attend regional track two meetings, but it has not yet hosted any national seminar for the public nor does it have a permanent staff for research and publication. There are indications that the institute may be reorganized and given a larger role both nationally and regionally. On the military side, the Ministry of Defense has not indicated if it too would sponsor any research institution other than its internal organizations for intelligence and information gathering.

3 Canada

In 2002, Canadian security policy was dominated by the political aftermath of the terrorist attacks in the United States on September 11, 2001. Domestically, Canada implemented a number of measures designed to increase internal security and thwart the activities of terrorist groups operating inside the country. In North America, Canada participated in a wide array of new and enhanced border and continental security arrangements with the United States. Abroad, Canada participated in the U.S.-led war on terrorism in Afghanistan. Yet, Canadian security policy continues to be characterized by remarkable continuity. The fundamental principles and interests that guide Canadian security policy have endured: pre-September 11 trends continue, and foremost is the persistent long-term neglect of the military capacities and monetary investments required for the maintenance of a relevant presence in world affairs. Canada's global profile has been in decline, a trend likely to continue in 2003 as political attention focuses on an internal leadership transition and domestic social and economic challenges. An exception to this official neglect will be continental security, because Canada must of necessity respond to the homeland security agenda in Washington. Canada is likely to join any U.S.-led coalition against Iraq, but its contribution will be limited by lukewarm political enthusiasm and weak military capabilities. Canada will most likely support an increasingly continental strategic approach as a function of the primacy of Canada's North American interests and its limited capacity to deliver abroad.

INTERNAL   Canada faces no immediate internal threats to its territorial integrity or domestic stability. While the issue of Quebec nationalism remains unresolved, separatism has been dormant for several years and is not expected to resurface in the near future. Internally, the implementation of anti-terrorism measures has priority as Canada seeks to fulfill its obligations and interest in preventing the country from being used by terrorists trying to attack the United States. An Anti-Terrorism Act, designed to strengthen law enforcement against the suspected 50 terrorist groups operating in Canada, and a Public Safety Act, designed to increase security in the civil airline sector, were introduced into Parliament.

Prime Minister Jean Chrétien's August 2002 announcement that he would step down in February 2004 and leave Parliament will focus domestic attention on transitional politics over the next year. Former Finance Minister Paul Martin is the leading candidate to replace Chrétien. With the ruling Liberal Party absorbed in a leadership struggle and Chrétien's "legacy" projects taking so much of available financial resources, foreign affairs and defense are unlikely to receive much political attention or new funding. The past year witnessed considerable turnover in senior government posts; among those new in their post are William (Bill) Graham as minister of foreign affairs, Susan Whelan as minister for international cooperation, John McCallum as minister of national defense, and David Kilgour as secretary of state (Asia Pacific). More turnovers in senior posts are expected before or when Chrétien departs office.

EXTERNAL   The Canadian government and public have become increasingly aware of the threat of future terrorist attacks in North America, although few believe Canada itself will be a direct target of such an attack. Even prior to September 11, Canadians had grown increasingly anxious about international instability and transnational threats, and this general anxiety persists. Regional conflicts, large-scale abuses of human rights, and participation in peacekeeping and intervention operations—all contribute to perceptions of a volatile world. In addition to the higher profile now accorded to terrorism, international criminal activities such as drug trafficking and money laundering reinforce the threat posed by non-state actors. Concerns over illegal migration have abated somewhat, but there is much deeper concern about the future of the global economy. The downturn in global markets in 2002 affected most Canadians directly, reducing the value of their investments and retirement savings. The economic crises and threat to democracy in South America, coming on the heels of the exposure of widespread fraud and accounting malpractice in corporate America and the numerous financial shocks and currency crises of the past few years, have left many Canadians suspicious or fearful of globalization. Meanwhile, the Canadian government is concerned about the slow progress toward increased trade liberalization in the World Trade Organization (WTO) and the Asia-Pacific Economic Cooperation (APEC) forum as well as about some highly visible trade disputes with Washington.

Despite and partly because of close ties with the United States, Canadian governmental and public opinion is deeply worried about the penchant for unilateralism on the part of U.S. President George W. Bush, the tactics used to pursue the "war on terrorism," U.S. policies in the Middle East, and the corresponding growth of anti-Americanism abroad. As a result, the sympathy and support Canadians extended to the United States after September 11 have begun to diminish, and the Bush administration is now seen as alienating allies and squandering the political capital gained in the wake of the attacks. The administration's perceived low regard for and downright hostility toward multilateral institutions is another sore point. Canada has long sought to build and maintain a multilateral, institutionalized, rules-based international order, in which it and other countries have a voice and some expectation of influence. Washington's current unilateralism and bilateralism are seen as threatening these institutions and forcing Canada to cooperate with the United States in isolation from the formal multilateralism championed by Canadian diplomacy.

The Canadian government regards the security environment in Asia as largely stable, but characterized by potential flashpoints that can flare into crisis with little warning. The renewal of the crisis over North Korea, the Taiwan issue, separatism in Indonesia, and continued tensions between India and Pakistan are all regarded as significant threats to the stability of the broader Asia Pacific region. Central Asia is an area of growing concern. Recent terrorist attacks in the Asia Pacific region, in particular the October 2002 bombings in Bali, have eroded much of the confidence Canadians placed in the safety of business and tourism in the region. Increasingly, Asia is seen as beset by a tide of social discontent, growing radicalism, and the potential for violence. In November 2002, Canada's embassy in the Philippines was closed for a month due to a security threat.

DEFENSE POLICIES AND ISSUES

Canada's defense policy remains based on the 1994 *White Paper on Defence*. A defense update is currently in progress, but is not expected to make significant departures from current policy. Canadian security is regarded as dependent on international peace and security, and, as a result, defense policy has emphasized engagement in multilateral operations to promote international peace and stability, preferably through multilateral institutions such as the United Nations or the North Atlantic Treaty Organization (NATO). Accordingly, military doctrine is focused on the maintenance of multipurpose, combat-capable maritime, land, and air forces capable of deploying and sustaining expeditionary operations in cooperation with allies. Special and growing emphasis is placed on operational and technological interoperability with the U.S. military.

A serious funding shortfall is the most important issue confronting Canadian defense policy. Despite recent modest increases, Canada's military budget is only US$7.7 billion, 1.1 percent of gross domestic product, or US$226 per capita, a legacy of the cuts of the 1990s. This has affected both equipment and manpower. There are doubts as to the ability of Canada's aging military equipment to meet the challenges of future military operations and the requirements of interoperability with allies. While some equipment remains capable, other major capital inventory, including combat aircraft, maritime helicopters, replenishment vessels, and airlift capacities are in desperate need of replacement. The air force has a dwindling number of operational fighter aircraft. The size of the Canadian military has shrunk by more than 30 percent in the last decade to an active regular force strength of 52,300. Most land force formations are well below authorized strength and rely on reservists or transfers from other units to reach a full complement for deployments. Some Canadian naval vessels lack the crew complement required for full operational status. The shrinking size of the military, especially the army, has reduced Canada's ability to deploy and sustain forces abroad. In East Timor, Ethiopia, Eritrea, and Afghanistan, Canadian ground units have been deployed for only one six-month rotation, in part due to the lack of available replacement formations.

The government continues to call upon a smaller, less capable military to maintain a very high operational tempo, involving numerous involvements in peacekeeping operations or wars. Critics maintain that the Canadian military is seriously under-funded relative to the demands that have been placed upon it. Both the U.S. ambassador to Canada and the secretary-general of NATO have urged increased defense spending, while similar calls have come from within Canada from the auditor general, a parliamentary committee, the command inspector, Land Force Command, of the Canadian forces, the chief of the defense staff, and numerous public commentators and policy think tanks. However, there is little expectation that spending will increase significantly in the immediate future, given the leadership transition politics. Indeed, the defense update under way is widely regarded as a tactic to stall until a new leadership is in place. All of this will result in a Canadian military increasingly relegated to continental defense and "niche" roles in future multilateral operations.

CONTRIBUTIONS TO REGIONAL AND GLOBAL SECURITY

Canada continues to be an important economic and security partner with the other countries of the Asia Pacific region. With APEC regarded as largely stagnant, Canada has sought to enhance its economic ties with the region through bilateral trade arrangements with targeted countries. Special emphasis has been placed on China and India. The Canadian government continues to employ the "Team Canada" formula, which involves the cooperation of the federal and provincial governments as well as business in trade missions throughout the region.

Canada continues to be engaged in the security dialogue in Asia at the official and track two levels. During a March 2002 visit to Canada by Director General Nakatani Gen of Japan's Defense Agency, the then Defense Minister Art Eggleton and Nakatani agreed to work together on peacekeeping operations and the war on terrorism, and to promote the exchange of officers from both countries. Canada also participated in a peacekeeping operations seminar with India and Malaysia that was sponsored by the Association of Southeast Asian Nations (ASEAN) and the ASEAN Regional Forum (ARF). Foreign Affairs Minister Bill Graham attended the ARF meeting and the 35th ASEAN Post-Ministerial Conference in Brunei Darussalam. Canada participated in the ARF workshop on improving cooperation against terrorism, held in Thailand April 17–19, 2002. The issues discussed at the workshop, including immigration cooperation and travel document fraud, were of special interest to Canada. At the track two level, Canada remained engaged in the North Pacific Working Group of the Council for Security

Cooperation in Asia Pacific (CSCAP) and hosted an APEC Business Advisory Council (ABAC) meeting in February 2002; in April 2002, a Canada-North Korea Association was formed by Canadian senators, businesspersons, academics, and church and humanitarian workers to promote education and friendly Canadian-North Korean relations.

Although the "human security" agenda championed by Canada no longer has the profile it once did, Canada continues to support development and peace-building efforts in Asia. Afghanistan is a focus of human security and peace-building efforts: Canada pledged Can$100 million (US$64 million at Can$1 = US$0.64) for reconstruction in Afghanistan at the Tokyo Conference in 2002. Other peace-building initiatives in Asia include Philippines-Canada Development Fund projects in Mindanao; reconstruction, development, and food aid assistance to Afghanistan; conversion of some Pakistani debt to Canada into funds for development programs; economic and educational support for Pakistani women and children; support for peace-building efforts in Sri Lanka; continued support for the reconstruction effort in East Timor and diplomatic recognition of that country; funding for the Mine Action Resource Center in Colombo, Sri Lanka; human needs projects in Vietnam; and judicial reform and education in the Philippines.

Outside the Asia Pacific region, North America has been the primary focus of Canada's international security cooperation. In cooperation with the United States, Canada has taken steps to enhance the security of North America from "asymmetric threats" in general and terrorism in particular. These steps include tighter immigration and refugee policies; the introduction of a new permanent resident card for recent immigrants; creation of an Air Transport Security Authority responsible for passenger screening and air marshals; enhanced technology and improved staffing levels at border crossings, improved screening of ships and maritime containers; and visa policy changes. In December 2001, Canada and the United States signed the Joint Statement of Cooperation on Border Security and Regional Migration Issues, providing for closer cooperation on screening incoming air passengers and biometric identification for documents, and the Smart Border Declaration to enhance security while facilitating cross-border commerce.

September 11 also led to an increase in already extensive Canada-U.S. defense cooperation in North America, including an initiative to allow military personnel to operate in each other's countries and discussion of a headquarters planning group for anti-terrorist contingency planning. Canada's border and North American security measures have been driven by U.S. pressure and Canada's need to maintain an open border. Critics worry that some of the measures are undermining Canada's sovereignty and policy independence, while supporters say that they are in Canada's interests and help maintain influence with its large neighbor. Canadian policies must walk a delicate tightrope in maintaining sovereignty, disagreeing with some aspects of U.S. policy, and remaining a valued and credible ally in Washington's eyes.

In Europe, Canada's diplomatic and security profile is eroding, despite the continued commitment of over 1,200 personnel to the NATO stabilization force in Bosnia. While membership in NATO remains a cornerstone of Canadian security policy, there are concerns about the future of NATO and Canada's relevance in the European continent.

Canada was a significant contributor to U.S.-led operations in Afghanistan, and the Canadian government made a major military commitment to the U.S.-led war on terrorism, contributing a battle group contingent of 850 light infantry and a naval task group (two frigates, a supply ship, and a destroyer) in the Arabian Sea. A third frigate is assigned to the U.S. carrier battle group also in the Arabian Sea. Canada has further provided tactical airlift and long-range patrol aircraft and Joint Task Force 2 (JTF-2) Special Forces troops in Afghanistan. Over 2,000 military personnel were committed at the height of the deployment. Four Canadians were killed by friendly fire from U.S. aircraft in April 2002. The light infantry contingent was withdrawn in July 2002, and JTF-2 personnel returned to Canada in November. These deployments disrupted routine activities such as naval exercises and ship visits, although Canadian warships visited Shanghai, Yokosuka, and Hong Kong in 2002. Canada also participated in the annual RIMPAC exercise, deploying three Maritime Coastal Defense Vessels (MCDV) and a long-range patrol submarine.

Canada has consistently pursued the development and strengthening of multilateral diplomacy and international institutions to maintain international peace and security. International stability is seen as a precondition of Canadian security. Canadian diplomacy seeks to maintain a distinct voice in world affairs, and joins with like-minded countries to influence and provide a counterweight to U.S. decision making. Canada continues to contribute to global security through engagement at the United Nations, although its troop contributions to UN operations have declined dramatically in recent years. At the Group of Eight Summit in Kananaskis, Prime Minister Chrétien hoped to establish a development and human security legacy in the form of an "Africa

Initiative." However, this initiative was partly undercut by the priorities of the Bush administration, which arrived with its own agenda. This added more tension to an already strained relationship between Chrétien and Bush. Canada continues to support development initiatives in an effort to promote human needs around the world: Canada has an Action Plan on Basic Education developed by the Canadian International Development Agency (CIDA) to meet the goals set at the World Education Forum in Senegal in April 2000; and Canada is committed to funding HIV/AIDS prevention and care in developing countries, including India and Pakistan. Canada continues to support human rights and democratization in Latin America through the Organization of American States (OAS). Canada is expected to continue with such efforts in the future, although the demands of security against terrorist threats in North America, the decline in Canada's military capacities, and the limited resources available for peace building and development are three factors that suggest a declining profile for Canada in world affairs and an increasing focus on continental concerns.

4 China

THE SECURITY ENVIRONMENT

INTERNAL   Internally, China faces no immediate serious threats nor
are there any on the horizon, but as a society in the midst of dynamic
socioeconomic change, Chinese society confronts daunting challenges.
These challenges will now be the responsibility of the so-called fourth
generation of leaders, since China is undergoing a leadership transition,
the smoothest in the history of the People's Republic of China (PRC).
President Jiang Zemin gave up his party post as general secretary to Vice
President Hu Jintao as anticipated at the 16th Chinese Communist Party
(CCP) Congress in November 2002. The Congress also selected a new
Central Committee, which in turn selected its Politburo. The Politburo
then elected a nine-member Standing Committee, which stands at the
pinnacle of party power in China. Symbolic of the major shift, except
for Hu, the other members are all new to the Standing Committee. Premier Zhu Rongi, People's Congress Chairman Li Peng, and other members of the Standing Committee also left their positions as leaders. As
China enters the year 2003, it is still going through the formal transition
period, which ends in March, when the People's Congress meets to
select a new president and premier as well as other high-level government officials.

The Party Congress featured Jiang's leadership accomplishments,
and he retained the important position of chair of the Central Military
Commission (CMC), for which there is no retirement period. Deng
Xiaoping had also retained this position after he had stepped down as
head of the CCP. No matter how long he maintains the chairmanship
of the CMC, clearly Jiang will enjoy great prestige and influence in his

retirement, but this will eventually evaporate as the new leadership assumes real power as well as the formal positions. In general, the smooth leadership transition reflects the increased institutionalization of CCP norms and rules, which provide the average Chinese increased confidence in the stability of the leadership.

All expectations are for continued policy stability in the coming years. The new leaders have actually served in top positions now for many years as protégés of the third generation, and the senior leadership appears to have a strong consensus on the basic features of internal and external policies. However, over the longer run, some major political, economic, and social changes are inevitable simply because of changes in personalities and the leadership challenges that China faces as the result of 20 years of reform, accelerated change with its entry into the World Trade Organization (WTO), and increased integration within the international community.

China is also economically stable, although not without some serious concerns. The growth rate is considerably below the unsustainable double-digit levels of the early 1990s, but China maintained 7 percent–8 percent growth through the period of the Asian economic crisis and even grew 7.3 percent in 2001 when the world economy was in recession. The 2002 growth rate was 8 percent, above the government's target for a 7 percent average economic growth in the first decade of the 21st century. To most Chinese analysts, this decade-long target appears attainable as the Chinese economy is making a successful transition from export-led to domestic-driven growth. According to Zhu and Zeng Peiyan, chairman of the State Development Planning Commission of the State Council, consumer spending now accounts for about 60 percent of national income, compared to 20 percent for public, private, and foreign investment, and 20 percent for exports. The consumer sector is particularly buoyant with booming purchases of houses, apartments, automobiles, computers, mobile phones, and for Internet and other services. Seventy-two percent of households in Beijing own their own houses or apartments, and there is ample scope for improvement. Automobile sales reached 3.25 million vehicles in 2002, an increase of 37.1 percent, and four-fifths of the buyers are private citizens rather than public or cooperative entities. China has become the world's largest telephone market with more than 400 million telephones. Moreover, the Chinese consumer revolution is expected to last for years as vast groups of Chinese have yet to enter the consumer market.

Another source of economic growth comes from government spending at various levels on infrastructure, such as highways, railways, airports, seaports, pipelines, water projects, and communication facilities. Foreign capital continues to flow at record levels into China—about US$52.74 billion in 2002. However, China is also facing some major economic challenges including unemployment, slow income growth for farmers, regional development inequities, weakness in the banking sector, a growing government budget deficit, and a deflationary threat. The impact of implementing the WTO agreements on the Chinese economic system, and especially the agricultural sector, remains uncertain.

Although there are no significant security threats to the Chinese state, the Eastern Turkistan Islamic Movement, a Xinjiang terrorist group, has been responsible for more than 200 violent incidents between 1990 and 2001. Over this decade, 162 people were killed and more then 440 wounded, including women and children of minority groups and Han Chinese. China is gratified that both the United Nations and the United States have now recognized this group as a terrorist organization.

Cross-Taiwan Strait relations are less bright than the internal situation of mainland China. Taiwan President Chen Shui-bian's reference to "one state on either side of the Strait" was seen in Beijing as simply confirming the mainland's long-standing belief that Chen seeks independence. Beijing has not and will not resume official contacts and talks with Taipei before its leaders unambiguously accept the one-China principle, Beijing's bottom line. However, mainland China will continue to encourage the growth of economic and social contacts, such as the Three Direct Links (trade, transportation, and postal services), as being in the basic interests of China and perhaps the most feasible means of achieving the reunification goal with Taiwan. As a result, the economic interdependence across the Strait continues to deepen and is already having important political ramifications.

EXTERNAL China's external security environment remains complicated and problematic. On the one hand, China is at peace with all countries in Asia and in the world. On the other hand, China's relations with some countries, most importantly the United States and Japan, are still troubled.

Outwardly, China's relations with the United States continue to improve. High-level visits between the two sides have increased. President

George W. Bush has visited China twice, and both the Chinese president and the vice president visited the United States in 2002. The two countries continue to cooperate on and coordinate matters concerning counter-terrorism. There are some common interests, although different approaches, on regional and global issues such as North Korea, South Asia, and Iraq, permitting a measure of cooperation even on these difficult and sensitive areas. Growing trade and economic ties also deepen the relationship.

However, the substance of Sino-U.S. relations has not changed since the terrorist attacks in the United States on September 11, 2001, despite improved atmospherics. The underlying strategic view of each state remains deeply suspicious of the other's intentions, limiting the scope of cooperation. There are major differences on Taiwan, human rights, religious freedom, missile defense, and trade. Many Chinese still regard the United States as an international hegemonic power and a threat to world peace and to China's security and national unity.

China's relations with Japan are still troubled by the issues of Yasukuni Shrine visits by Japanese officials and references in Japanese textbooks to Japan's prewar and wartime role in China and disputes regarding small territorial and economic zones in the East China Sea. Although these may not directly affect China's security, they are fundamental in the perceptions, emotions, and public discourse between the two countries.

China's relations with Russia, the two Koreas, and Southeast and South Asian countries are proceeding smoothly. China and Russia established a working group on counter-terrorism in December 2001, which has met a number of times. The Association of Southeast Asian Nations (ASEAN) countries and China continue their efforts to build the world's largest free-trade zone by 2010. They also signed an accord on the South China Sea, promising not to take actions disruptive of the status quo in the region.

DEFENSE POLICIES AND ISSUES

China is improving political, economic, security, and military relations with Asia Pacific countries. It has regular security dialogues or consultations with Russia, Japan, India, Australia, and the United States. Defense ministers and military leaders of China and other Asian countries have frequently exchanged visits in recent years. Ships from China's navy pay friendly visits to ports in Japan, India, and Southeast Asian countries.

China continues to oppose missile defense although the government has toned down its opposition. There are also few public statements from China regarding the American military presence in Asia or the U.S.-Japan security alliance. The Chinese government accepts the U.S. military presence in Asia as a historical legacy and does not want to change the status quo. At the same time, China naturally reacts to what appear to be efforts to strengthen the U.S. presence and to interfere with China's sovereignty or interests, for example, in Taiwan.

The Chinese government continues to support U.S. efforts against terrorism in Afghanistan and elsewhere. However, many Chinese military officers and experts as well as the general public worry that a permanent American military presence in Afghanistan and Central Asia may threaten China's security on its western borders.

DEFENSE SPENDING   China's People's Congress, held in March 2002, allocated 167.03 billion yuan (US$20.04 billion at 1 yuan = US$0.12) for military spending, an increase of 252 million yuan (US$30.24 million) or 17.6 percent over the previous year's level. The increase reportedly was needed to protect national sovereignty and territorial integrity, enhance technological capabilities, and increase personnel salaries and pensions.

ARMS CONTROL   China is increasingly active in arms control, both in international negotiations and in national implementation of China's commitments. There has been increasing recognition of the importance of controlling the transfer of weapons to unstable regions, even when those are far from China itself. China is in the process of drafting laws, issuing regulations and laws, and identifying items, such as missile and missile technology and chemical, biological, and military goods, that are subject to export controls. The new rules require that exporters be registered and exports of sensitive goods be approved by government regulatory agencies.

CONTRIBUTIONS TO REGIONAL AND GLOBAL SECURITY

As part of its effort to maintain a stable security environment, China promotes peace and nation building in its immediate periphery. Its principal interests are in Korea, Central Asia, Afghanistan, South Asia, and ASEAN.

In the case of the Korean peninsula, China supports North Korea's efforts to improve its relations with the South, Japan, and the United States and encourages North Korean economic reform, including the development of a special economic zone across the Yalu River from China. China continues to provide oil, coal, electricity, grain, and fertilizer to North Korea to help the people overcome their economic difficulties and maintain a stable society. The Chinese leaders and Foreign Ministry officials have restated China's position concerning the nuclear issue on the peninsula: China insists that the Korean peninsula should be a nuclear-free area; it does not support nuclear weapons on the peninsula, and it opposes North Korea's withdrawal from the Nonproliferation Treaty (NPT). At the same time, China does not support sanctions or military action against the North. It believes that discussions and negotiations can resolve the issues related to North Korea's nuclear weapons and missile programs. China stands willing to work with all relevant parties, including North and South Korea, the United States, Japan, and Russia, to find a peaceful resolution to the nuclear threat on the peninsula. Intensive contacts continue between China and other parties on the issue.

In Central Asia, China took a significant step in June 2001, when the presidents of six countries—China, Russia, Kazakhstan, the Kyrgyz Republic, Tajikistan, and Uzbekistan—held a summit meeting in Shanghai and launched the Shanghai Cooperation Organization (SCO) as a new regional body designed to promote peace, stability, and economic and trade ties. In June 2002, the SCO agreed to establish an anti-terrorism center in Bishkek, capital of Kyrgyz. The center will "serve as the legal basis to start substantial cooperation in security issues and offer a more effective means for the fledging organization to combat terrorism together." The member states are also negotiating agreements for multinational cooperation in the fight against illegal arms smuggling, drug trafficking, illegal migration, and other criminal activities. The six foreign ministers of SCO issued another statement against terrorism on the first anniversary of September 11.

China is also strengthening bilateral ties with Central Asian countries. For example, Kyrgyz and China conducted joint two-day anti-terrorism military exercises in the border regions of the two countries in October 2002. Some 300 troops and more than ten tanks and helicopters from both countries participated in the exercises that staged hypothetical attacks by terrorists. The two countries exchanged information, made joint decisions, and finally "killed" all the terrorists. This is said to be the first time the two countries have held bilateral military exercises within the framework of the SCO, and also the first time for the Chinese army to conduct a live ammunition war-game with a foreign army. The Chinese military plans to have more joint counter-terrorist military exercises with SCO member countries in the near future.

China has a special interest in supporting the new Afghan government and its state-building processes. China hosted Afghan leader Hamid Karzai in early 2002, and President Jiang met President Karzai again in June when both leaders attended a meeting in Central Asia. After the Chinese embassy in Kabul reopened, Chinese Foreign Minister Tang Jiaxuan and Vice Minister Wang Yi visited Afghanistan. In the May 15, 2002, meeting between President Karzai and Minister Tang, Tang assured the Afghan government that China's only purpose is to help the country develop and maintain peace. During the visit, China also offered to send Chinese to direct repairs of the Republic Hospital in Kabul and medical facilities in other cities. In addition, Chinese leaders offered to study water projects; provide police uniforms and office materials for 80,000 Afghan officials; provide agricultural technology to help replace poppy fields; and accept visa applications and encourage the exchange of visits between the two countries. Both countries signed three agreements related to economic and technological cooperation between them during the visit.

When Karzai visited China, China also promised US$150 million for rebuilding Afghanistan and US$1 million in cash for administrating the new government, with more assistance promised in the future. According to Sun Yuxi, the Chinese ambassador to Afghanistan, the US$150 million assistance will comprise two parts. The first part will be designated for infrastructure such as water and power plants, hospitals, schools, transportation and communication facilities; the second part will go to production facilities in mining and other industries. Some of the goods, such as food and medicine, have been delivered to Afghanistan. More than 14 planes and 30 trucks carrying materiel came from China following an earthquake in Afghanistan in March 2002. These provisions included medicine and medical equipment for 14 hospitals and goods for schools and 32 Afghanistan governmental organizations, including the president's office. The Chinese government encourages its companies to invest in Afghanistan and to participate in the country's reconstruction.

In the subcontinent, China pursues a balanced policy with Pakistan and India, refusing to support one side against the other, as in the past. This policy has been made clear to both countries. China has assisted in diplomatic efforts to prevent conflict; in January 2002, for example, the Premier Zhu visited India at the height of Indo-Pakistani tensions and urged restraint and a peaceful resolution.

In Southeast Asia, China has become more active in the ASEAN Regional Forum (ARF) and regional multilateral security approaches. Foreign Minister Tang stressed the "nontraditional security" issues at the Foreign Ministers Meeting of ARF in Brunei in July 2002. He called for more dialogue and cooperation on these issues in ARF, ASEAN + 3 (China, Japan, and South Korea), and other regional entities. He also praised the three documents of preventive diplomacy accepted at the ARF meeting. China provided a position paper on a new security concept to the ARF Foreign Ministers Meeting. China would like to see more defense officials and military personnel participating in the ARF process.

5 European Union

THE SECURITY ENVIRONMENT

Europe's security outlook is being shaped by several distinct recent trends. First, as the United States has broadened its war on terrorism to include "evil" states, especially Iraq, and placed pressure on its allies for support, European responses have become individualistic and rarely collective. This "re-nationalization" of European foreign policies is quite in contrast to other integrative efforts. Second, and also in response to the September 11, 2001, attacks in the United States but beginning earlier, Europe's security outlook has been shifting significantly inward toward integration of anti-terrorism and domestic security policies. With the establishment of an "area of freedom, justice, and security" at the Tampere Council meeting in October 1999, the European Union (EU) has taken several important steps—the creation of a European arrest warrant, a common definition of terrorism, strengthened cooperation among police (EUROPOL) and magistrates (EUROJUST)—to improve its anti-terrorism capabilities. In this context, and in marked contrast to the transatlantic differences in other areas, the European Union is collaborating closely and effectively with U.S. law enforcement agencies. Third, the European Union is continuing to emphasize regional integration as a key instrument to prevent conflict and to build peace in war-torn societies. Two important steps were taken in 2002: (1) deepening the European Union itself by establishing a European Convention that will present proposals on institutional reform and streamlining treaties in 2003 and (2) admitting Central and East European nations beginning in 2004.

These trends and the lessons of cooperative military action in the

Balkans and Afghanistan are establishing a new but yet undeclared transatlantic division of labor in which the European Union takes a (more or less) supportive role both before and after U.S.-dominated military action. This pattern has already been demonstrated along the European Union's own periphery in the Balkans and is being extended to other regions. It encourages a further broadening of Europe's security outlook, but has not affected much of Europe's involvement in Asian security affairs. So far, Europe's security priorities remain with stabilizing its own periphery and ending the spiraling violence in the Near and Middle East, where the European Union operates within the framework of the Middle East Quartet (the United Nations, the United States, Russia, and the European Union).

Fragmentation and re-nationalization continue to hamper European foreign and security policies. This has been particularly evident on approaches toward preventing the proliferation of weapons of mass destruction, where U.S. determination to move forcefully, and even to take preemptive military action, has greatly increased the stakes for Europeans in their association with the United States. In the immediate aftermath of the September 11 attacks, European governments were united in supporting U.S. President George W. Bush's war on terrorism, although with distinct national colors. But as U.S. attention increasingly moved from al Qaeda to Iraq, diverging views came to the fore, most notably just before the German federal elections when Chancellor Gerhard Schroeder criticized the U.S. administration for seeking to shift the approach from containment and UN inspections to "regime change" without consultation with its allies. Schroeder both alienated the Bush administration and undermined the chances of a common European approach toward the Iraq problem. Continuing disunity in Europe means that the European Union's ability to act decisively during periods of crisis on external security issues is highly limited, even when that action is restricted to nonmilitary actions. For Asia Pacific, as for the world at large, a united European role is largely confined to situations that have global (and thus European) implications, such as the situation on the Korean peninsula, and to the earlier stages of preventive diplomacy or to post-conflict economic assistance and peacekeeping. Although Europe's capacity for initiative is not great, Europe and its major constituent states, two of which are permanent members of the UN Security Council, are essential partners in building regional and global order, including security, trade, and environmental regimes.

DEFENSE POLICIES AND ISSUES

DEFENSE POLICIES   Despite recent institutional advances, Europe is a long way from a common foreign, security, and defense policy. National differences on how independent Europe's policies should be from those of its alliance partners may prevent a common policy from ever emerging. While there is a common ambition to create more coherent positions and capabilities, fiscal constraints also militate against implementation. As a consequence of this expectation-capability gap, EU member states have come to embrace, some reluctantly, a functionally and geographically circumscribed role for the European Union as an international power.

Functionally, the EU role has a distinct "civilian" taint. To begin with, since the Gothenburg summit in summer 2001, the European Union has put the establishment of common conflict prevention measures on an equal footing with the strengthening of military crisis management capabilities. In line with this, the European Union itself assumed the command of the International Police Task Force in early 2002 in Bosnia and Herzegovina, and it will also lead the Task Force Fox—supporting the implementation of the Macedonian Peace Process—in the near future. In central Asia, 13 of 15 EU member states participated in the International Security Assistance Force (ISAF) mission in Afghanistan, and several of them committed (special) combat forces to support U.S. troops fighting al Qaeda and Taliban forces. As several member countries made clear at the crucial post-September 11 Laeken EU summit meeting, they do not foresee any combined EU military mission in crisis management in the foreseeable future.

This political commitment is also reflected in European arms procurement policies. Even if member states reach all headline goals for the European Rapid Reaction Force (ERRF) by 2003, this force will not be operational for the full range of peacekeeping and enforcement missions envisioned by the organizers. France and the United Kingdom increased their defense spending considerably in 2002, but European military establishments will continue to lack vital capabilities in the years to come in the fields of battle-space management (command, control, communications, intelligence, surveillance, and reconnaissance), battle-space action (e.g., precision strike assets), and transportation and force integration engaging in large-scale power projection. When it comes to fighting wars, Europe can only contribute small "pockets of excellence" to U.S.-led military operations while engaging in pre- and post-conflict management.

Geographically, the European Union still favors a "Europe plus periphery" perimeter approach. The integration of transforming democracies in Central and Eastern Europe, the stabilization of the Balkan countries, and the continued political and financial support for conflict management in Israel and Palestine remain the most important EU foreign policy projects. At the same time, in 2002 member states individually or combined enlarged their respective perimeter of military action in Operation Enduring Freedom with patrolling activities in the Arabian Sea and rear support in Central and South Asia.

DEFENSE BUDGETS   Despite recent increases in defense spending by several EU members states (see table 1), real European defense spending in U.S. dollar terms is expected to decline. Public deficits and the stringent fiscal limits imposed by the European Union's own Stability and Growth Pact continue to constrain defense spending. The EU states are seeking to offset these by restructuring European defense industries to allow more efficient resource allocation and, somewhat reluctantly, by increasing the share of the common budget (as opposed to national budgets) in funding EU military actions. But these largely cosmetic steps will not prevent the transatlantic defense spending gap from widening further. Germany announced in October 2002 that budget constraints will not permit it to boost its budget by €600 million (US$624 million at €1 = US$1.04) for a special anti-terrorism fund, and France may follow suit in 2003. Thus, only the United Kingdom's planned 1.2 percent real growth rate (2002–2005/06) of its annual defense budget will enable its armed forces to conduct large-scale integrated military operations with the United States.

Table 1. Defense Expenditures in the European Union (US$ billion)

Country	2001 Defense Expenditure	% of GDP (2001)	2001 Defense Budget	2002 Defense Budget
France	32.2	2.6	25.8	29.5
United Kingdom	34.7	2.5	23.5	24.2
Germany	26.9	1.5	21.5	24.9
Italy	21.0	2.0	15.9	19.4
Spain	6.9	1.2	7.1	8.4
Netherlands	6.3	1.7	5.7	6.6

SOURCE: International Institute for Strategic Studies, *The Military Balance*, 2002/2003.

ARMS SALES   Europe's share in the Asian arms market has been on the rise since the mid-1990s. This development can be explained not just by the continued appetite for arms in Asia but also by the loosening of restrictions on sales in Europe. Several factors are involved, including the relaxation of more restrictive national legal frameworks for arms exports by the Europeanization of the defense industry and the pressures created by the war against terrorism and the subsequent coalition-building effort. As an example of the first, the 2000 EU Code of Conduct on Arms Exports as well as a six-nation Framework Agreement "Concerning Measures to Facilitate the Restructuring and Operation of the European Defense Industry" (Germany, France, Italy, Spain, Sweden, and the United Kingdom) leave some space for a new interpretation of security, foreign policy, development, and human rights concerns when deciding on country white lists and common export guidelines. Pressure to contribute to the coalition against terrorism is reflected in the lifting of the EU arms export embargo against the Northern Alliance during the Afghan war and the French decision to resume military ties with Pakistan, both policy changes occurring in November 2001. Competition with the highly aggressive export policies of the United States also drives Europeans to reduce arms sales restrictions.

CONTRIBUTIONS TO REGIONAL AND GLOBAL SECURITY

DEPLOYMENTS IN ASIA AND THE PACIFIC   As discussed, EU contributions to regional and global security stress diplomatic and economic components, not military components. This is particularly true of Asia and the Pacific. In contrast to the United States, the European Union's military presence in the Asia Pacific region is negligible, confined to special cases originating in the colonial era. France and the United Kingdom are the only EU member states to have troop deployments. Whereas France has a permanent troop presence in its Pacific territories (some 5,200 soldiers, two frigates, plus support ships, aircraft, and helicopters), the United Kingdom has stationed about 1,100 Gurkha troops in Brunei Darussalam with the support of the sultanate. The United Kingdom continues to be a member of the Five Power Defense Arrangements (FPDA) with Australia, Malaysia, New Zealand, and Singapore.

CONFLICT SITUATIONS   In recent years, economic relations have been the focal point of most European policies toward Asia. In the post-September 11 environment, this has changed in two ways. Security and terrorism are at the fore, and with this new emphasis, there is a decided shift in attention from Northeast Asia to Southeast Asia, and South and Central Asia, with the Korean peninsula as a partial exception. These trends are documented in the second Asia Concept Paper of the German government, published with some delay in June 2002, which places greater emphasis on security issues by recognizing that most of the world's trouble spots lie in Asia (India-Pakistan, the Korean peninsula, the Taiwan Strait, and the South China Sea). With regard to the war on terrorism, most European nations have broadened their political, financial, and military engagement in Afghanistan, but only France has stationed forces in Central Asia on a more than temporary basis.

Anti-terrorism continues to have priority, reinforced in the past year by terrorist attacks involving French defense technicians in Karachi in May 2002 and the Bali bombings in October, in which some European tourists lost their lives. However, EU-Asian anti-terrorism cooperation, although begun in earnest at the September 2001 gathering of the Asia-Europe Meeting (ASEM), continues to lag behind transatlantic cooperation. In April 2002, ASEM senior officials in justice and home affairs met to discuss terrorism, and in June, ASEM foreign ministers discussed a Chinese initiative to strengthen anti-terrorist information exchanges. On September 23 in Copenhagen, ASEM leaders issued a Declaration on Cooperation against International Terrorism and established an informal consultative mechanism of ASEM coordinators to react to "significant international events." In 2003, ASEM will sponsor one conference in Beijing on anti-terrorism measures, and a conference on money laundering will be held in Germany.

The European Union continues its commitment to the Korean peace process, although it is playing a less prominent role than in 2001. All member states, except France and Ireland—and the European Union itself—established diplomatic relations with North Korea after the ASEM 2000 Summit Meeting in Seoul. Accordingly, individual countries (the United Kingdom, Sweden, and Germany) as well as the EU troika have tried to prod Pyongyang toward greater cooperation with the outside world, especially South Korea. At their 2002 meeting in Copenhagen, ASEM leaders endorsed efforts by South Korea and Japan to further the dialogue with the North.

Europe's lower profile toward the Korean peninsula this year has also been evident in its policy on the Korean Peninsula Energy Development

Organization (KEDO). Some European leaders criticized President Bush for including Pyongyang in the so-called axis of evil in January 2002, but there was no European comment in April when Washington decided not to certify North Korean compliance with the provisions of the Agreed Framework. Given North Korea's later admission of a uranium enrichment program, this implicit support for the more hard-nosed U.S. approach may have been the right course. Following the admission, Javier Solana, the European Union's defense and foreign policy coordinator, quickly termed the Agreed Framework invalid, possibly helping heal some misunderstandings with Washington. But it also suggested the priority that Washington has in Brussels in comparison to the Asian KEDO board members, Japan and South Korea, which were inclined to take a more cautious approach. Europe continues to provide large amounts of food aid and other assistance to North Korea and supports inter-Korean reconciliation. However, the crisis over North Korea's weapons of mass destruction (WMD) programs has wider implications for the international order, and thereby must be addressed by Europe in a broader than local or regional context.

Europe is deepening its financial, political, and military involvement in post-Taliban Afghanistan. In December 2001, Germany hosted the Afghan Peace Conference. In January 2002, the European Union and its member states pledged some 30 percent of all promised aid at the International Conference on the Reconstruction of Afghanistan in Tokyo. Germany and the Netherlands are taking over the ISAF command in early 2003.

In contrast to the Korean peninsula and Afghanistan, other important Asian security issues, including the Indian-Pakistani conflict, received little European attention. In the Indian-Pakistani case, the United Kingdom actively supports U.S. diplomatic efforts to prevent an outbreak of hostilities, but neither EU members nor the European Union itself played any visible role.

MULTILATERAL SECURITY   The European Union contributes to regional peace and stability in the Asia Pacific region through various regional and international bodies. In 2002, Javier Solana participated for the third time in the ASEAN Regional Forum (ARF) Foreign Ministers Meeting in Brunei Darussalam in July, where member states signed a joint declaration on enhanced anti-terrorist cooperation. At the ASEM leaders meeting in Copenhagen, the European Union and Asian nations joined in stressing that the fight against terrorism must be based on the principles of the UN charter and basic norms of international law. In addition, the ASEM Copenhagen Declaration on Cooperation against International Terrorism underscored that the fight against terrorism requires a comprehensive approach involving political, economic, diplomatic, legal, and military means. This offers a slightly different emphasis than the Bush administration, which is perceived in both regions as stressing the military component. However, there are few if any indications that European and Asian UN Security Council members are in closer cooperation in their efforts to influence the United States.

The European Union continues to contribute about 40 percent of total UN expenditures for peacekeeping operations. In the past, EU member states have been heavily involved in UN peacekeeping operations in East Asia, notably through the International Force in East Timor (INTERFET) and the UN Transitional Administration in East Timor (UNTAET). In 2002, the European Union continued to strongly support the transition process by sending election monitors (in April), participating in the UN Mission of Support in East Timor (UNMISET) (in May), and issuing a long-term assistance strategy (2002–2006) that focuses on improving health care and rural development.

ECONOMIC ASSISTANCE   The European Union and its member states account for about half of global Official Development Assistance (ODA). In Asia Pacific, the European Union continues to be the second most important source of ODA after Japan, although the latter still disburses roughly twice as much ODA to Asia Pacific. As most EU development assistance is disbursed through bilateral programs, national financial constraints resulting from the stringent criteria of the Stability and Growth Pact will almost certainly negatively impact the ODA performance of EU members. Europe continues to be an important source of investment capital and markets for many Asia Pacific countries, although this fact is still often overshadowed by the predominance of national (as opposed to EU) statistical information.

6 India

THE SECURITY ENVIRONMENT

India's security outlook for 2003 and beyond has only somewhat improved over last year's bleak outlook. The year 2002 began with the Indian armed forces mobilized and confronting the Pakistani army along the entire 3,244-kilometer international border and Line of Control (LC) in the west and in Jammu and Kashmir. Terrorism and proxy war continued through the year, and on at least two occasions war between the two nuclear-armed powers seemed imminent. The international community was united in counseling restraint, but the deployments continued until mid-December 2002, when both sides withdrew their forces, although only from the international border. With war clouds on the horizon farther west and cross-border terrorism continuing, a re-escalation of tensions and potential for conflict in the subcontinent remain very high.

INTERNAL The political situation remains stable as the governing coalition government at the center faces no serious or immediate challenges from within or from the opposition. Prime Minister Atal Bahari Vajpayee remains popular with a high approval rating for his leadership. There is speculation that he has health problems, but this is hotly denied by official spokespersons. Lal Krishna Advani, a senior leader of the Bharatiya Janata Party (BJP, or Indian People's Party), and also the home minister, was appointed the deputy prime minister in June and is in a strong position to succeed, if required.

Tensions remain from the serious communal clashes in early 2002 in the western state of Gujarat, among the very few states ruled by the

BJP. The violence was precipitated when a Muslim mob set a railway compartment on fire, killing 59 Hindu activists returning from a pilgrimage. This led to a widespread outbreak of retaliatory violence around the province, which the state government was unable and, according to some reports, unwilling to control. Some 1,000 people died, mostly Muslims. The inaction of the chief minister and the limitations of the state administration came under severe criticism from independent authorities and autonomous commissions. Opposition political parties strongly urged the chief minister's removal and imposition of central rule over the state, which the central government rejected. The BJP rebounded in the crucial mid-December elections in Gujarat, achieving a convincing majority. The BJP success in these elections is likely to portend a shift toward a more strident expression of Hindu nationalism by the ruling party in key state elections during 2003 and through national parliamentary elections in mid-2004. The coming years are likely to witness a major contest between secular and pro-Hindutva forces in the country.

Internal security remains a serious concern. Cross-border terrorism continues across the LC in Jammu and Kashmir. A strike by terrorists on an army camp in the southern part of the province in May 2002 killed 34 persons, mainly wives and children of soldiers, leading to heightened tension along the LC. There has been a spate of other terrorist actions across the state and elsewhere, notably the attacks on Hindu temples at Gujarat and Jammu that killed several dozen persons in each temple. Elections were held in Jammu and Kashmir in September and October under unprecedented security. Still terrorists succeeded in killing a state minister and 82 other candidates and political workers. In spite of this, the elections were conducted successfully with an unexpectedly high 44 percent of the total electorate voting. A new government has been formed in the state by a coalition of the Congress Party and the People's Democratic Party, a provincial Muslim party. The election demonstrated dissatisfaction with the long-established local leadership. With the new government in place, the coming year may see some progress toward stability and normalization in Jammu and Kashmir.

Low-level law and order issues trouble northeast India, north central India, and areas adjacent to Nepal. Some tension arose between two southern states over the sharing of river waters, exposing the vulnerability of the country to natural resource depletion, perhaps an increasingly likely trend in the future.

India's economy has grown steadily, recording a gross domestic product growth of 4.8 percent for the fiscal year ending March 2002, and an estimated 5.8 percent for the following year, demonstrating the dynamism of the Indian economy despite international tensions and volatility. Nevertheless, economic reforms and particularly third-generation liberalization policies have not kept pace with expectations. Consequently, international credit ratings were lowered early in 2002, and foreign direct investment stagnated at a low level. The information technology (IT) industry, however, has bounced back despite the global recession and is expected to grow significantly in 2003. The long-term economic outlook is cloudy, depending on the government's political will and ability to restructure the economy, reduce bureaucratic control, eliminate governmental ownership of industries, develop infrastructure, and attract foreign direct investment. The record on these items is not so positive as to warrant a growth rate above 6 percent in 2003.

EXTERNAL   India's foreign policy objective is to strive for a stable and peaceful international environment focusing particularly on India's immediate neighborhood. Countering international and domestic terrorism remain high-priority tasks for the government for the foreseeable future.

In the war against terrorism, India strongly supports the U.S.-led effort, considers UN Resolution 1373 the proper guideline for countering global terrorism, and urges international cooperation for the resolution's effective implementation. New Delhi remains deeply concerned about the spillover of terrorism from Afghanistan through Pakistani-held territory into India. The government estimates that in spite of U.S. pressures and assurances by Pakistan's president, there has been no reduction in cross-border terrorism from this source. New Delhi believes that terrorism must be eradicated without bias wherever it exists and remains determined to take all necessary steps to crush it decisively to preserve India's own security and territorial integrity as well as to protect the country's citizens.

Because of the terrorist problem, relations with Pakistan remained strained throughout the year. The Indian high commissioner was recalled in December 2001 and the Pakistani high commissioner in New Delhi was asked to leave in May 2002, although diplomatic relations continued with reduced staffs. Train and bus links were cut off and remain so, and civil airline overflights have not resumed. India is firmly committed to a resumption of the bilateral dialogue process with

Pakistan in accordance with the 1972 Simla Agreement and the 1999 Lahore Declaration. Once Pakistan successfully follows through on its own commitment to stop cross-border terrorism, India is ready to resume the composite eight-track dialogue process with Islamabad that was initiated in 1997. But from New Delhi's perspective, developments in Pakistan have been discouraging at best. The Pakistan elections of October 2002, which the European Commission observers called seriously flawed, saw the rise of a coalition of six Islamic parties, which helped form governments in two provinces. The coalition's influence in Islamabad has grown, portending a major shift toward Islamization unless stringent measures are taken to check it.

Except for Pakistan, India's relations with other South Asian neighbors remain cordial and friendly, despite the difficult internal situations in most of them. India supports Sri Lanka's promising efforts at peace and dialogue with the Liberation Tigers of Tamil Eelam (LTTE) and welcomed the Oslo agreement in early December. India believes that a negotiated settlement should meet the aspirations of all elements of Sri Lankan society. Regular security-related dialogues continue with Myanmar. Cooperation in building roads along the border and plans to enhance port facilities within Myanmar are in progress. India has played an active role in all internationally sponsored meetings on Afghanistan's reconstruction and rehabilitation. India provided an initial line of credit of US$100 million, which was later converted into a grant, and then supplemented it with another grant of US$10 million. There have been frequent visits by Afghanistan's ministers to India throughout the year.

Aside from Pakistan, India's two biggest concerns in its neighborhood in the immediate future are the Maoist insurgency in Nepal and the possibility of the spread of Islamic extremism in Bangladesh. In Nepal, the insurgency complicates an already troubled situation in a country of strategic importance to India with a serious potential to destabilize the entire region. In Bangladesh, law and order problems and terrorist activities are growing. New Delhi has expressed deep concern about the presence of senior al Qaeda activists in Bangladesh, which Dhaka has denied.

Relations with China continue to improve. Premier Zhu Rongji paid an official visit January 13–17, 2002. Six memorandums of understanding or agreements were signed, including ones concerning cooperation on science and technology, outer space, and promotion of tourism. The two sides established a bilateral dialogue mechanism against terrorism.

It was agreed to expedite the process of clarification and confirmation of the Line of Actual Control (LAC) along the India-China border, although there was not much progress in the 14th Joint Working Group meeting held in November 2002 in New Delhi. Senior-level visits of political, business, and military leaders of both countries are increasing. India-China trade grew by about 26 percent during 2002–2003 and is likely to exceed US$4.5 billion. Direct New Delhi–Beijing air services were established for the first time in March 2002. At the same time, India notes the ongoing modernization of the People's Liberation Army as well as China's annual double-digit defense spending increases. New Delhi is also concerned about the continued transfer of missile parts and components technology to Pakistan. Nevertheless, there are high expectations that when Prime Minister Vajpayee visits China in 2003 progress will be made in the overall relationship and on the specific and important issue of the demarcation of the LAC.

Relations with Southeast Asia continue to be close due to a common historical legacy, cultural affinities, and recently enhanced commercial and economic interaction. The resilience of the Indian economy and closer political and economic engagement have given these relations new energy, which is likely to intensify in the years ahead. Terrorism in Southeast Asia and terrorism's cross-border nature have lent an urgency to developing still closer cooperation to curb such activities, and this cooperation is likely to grow, especially with Singapore.

India and Russia share the vision of a strategic partnership in the 21st century, and high-level visits symbolic of the traditional close ties between the two countries continue. A strategic dialogue between Russian and Indian national security councils was held early in 2002. The most important event of 2002 was the visit of Russia's President Vladimir Putin to India in December, ending a period of nine years since the last visit of a Russian president to the country. The leaders issued a Delhi Declaration intended to elevate the strategic partnership to an even higher and qualitatively new level. They also agreed to strengthen economic, scientific, and technological cooperation. However, trade between the two countries remains very low, except for defense-related items.

Driven by common concerns about terrorism and growing economic and human ties, relations with the United States continue to strengthen. More frequent and high-level meetings took place in 2002 than in the previous 50 years. Though some of these meetings focused on defusing the crisis with Pakistan, they also helped build bilateral cooperation. Countering international terrorism is high on the agenda. Specific assistance and cooperation include intelligence sharing, assistance in investigations in terrorist attacks, and logistics support in Operation Enduring Freedom in Afghanistan. In 2002, Washington took a stronger position on terrorism against India and condemned all recent terrorist attacks on the country. Bilateral counter-terrorism cooperation has been strengthened to prevent acts of terrorism and eradicate terrorist groups. It was decided to institutionalize the entire range of cooperation in the security area under a new "strategic framework dialogue." A number of activities have already taken place under this framework. This includes the India-U.S. Defense Policy Group, which decided to resume the Service to Service Steering Groups and then set up a military coordination group to promote military exchanges. Measures are also being taken to strengthen technical cooperation in defense production and supplies. A dialogue between the U.S. Joint Chiefs of Staff and India's newly created Integrated Defense Staff is envisaged as well as dialogue between different geographic operational commands. The outlines of a long-term strategic relationship between the two countries are in place and substantive interactions are likely to grow in the near future.

DEFENSE POLICIES AND ISSUES

DEFENSE POLICY   India's defense policy is geared toward defending the country's borders as defined by law, protecting the lives and properties of citizens against terrorism, and maintaining a credible minimum deterrent against the use or the threat of use of weapons of mass destruction. New Delhi also propagates cooperation and understanding with neighboring countries, developing confidence-building measures and pursuing security and strategic dialogue with major powers and key interlocutors. India will continue its policy on disarmament based on the principles of supreme national interest, nondiscrimination, universality, and equal security for all. India's military doctrine is to maintain a dissuasive defense capability against all potential aggressors, and to back this up with both a conventional as well as strategic deterrent capability should the former fail. The country's first joint Strategic Forces Command will come into being in January 2003 and will be headed by an air force officer with three-star rank. This command will handle all nuclear assets and set up an elaborate structure to deal with all contingencies.

DEFENSE BUDGET   India's defense budget rose by 14 percent over the revised budget of the previous year. But as the revised budget actually was scaled down from the estimated budget, due to the inability of the Ministry of Defense to spend the sanctioned amount, the increase is misleading. By current U.S. dollar value, the defense budget actually went down from the previous year, due to the devaluation of the rupee. The rupee increase in the budget is required to support additional forces in high altitude, to acquire new weapons systems, and for increased expenditure in counter-terrorism operations in Jammu and Kashmir. The bulk of this increase will go to meet the expenses of the prolonged border deployment of the armed forces for almost all of 2002. The budget does not support large-scale force modernization. Table 1 reflects the

Table 1: India's Defense Budget (in billions of Indian rupees)

	1999–2000	2000–2001	2001–2002	2002–2003
Army	275.67	278.78	330.00	350.11
Air Force	102.43	106.11	120.00	156.89
Navy	68.37	73.85	87.00	98.72
Research and development	28.24	33.42	33.23	36.56
Defense production	−4.01	4.05	0.16	7.71
Total	470.71	496.22	570.00	650.00

SOURCE: Indian Ministry of Defense Annual Report presented to Parliament on February 28, 2002.
NOTE: The value of the Indian rupee at the time of presentation of the budget was approximately Rs 48 = US$1. The total defense budget was US$13.54 billion.

details of expenditures for the last four years. A steady increase in the defense expenditure is likely to continue in the future, keeping pace with the growth of the economy, the need for modernization, and the development of strategic deterrence.

FORCE STRUCTURE AND ACQUISITIONS   Indian armed forces total 1.3 million personnel, with 1.1 million in the army, 150,000 in the air force, and 50,000 in the navy. There are about 3,500 medium tanks, 4,500 artillery pieces, and 2,500 air-defense guns. The army aviation has about 120 helicopters and a variety of surveillance radars, drones, and surface-to-air missiles. The air force has about 774 combat aircraft and 34 armed helicopters. These are divided into 38 combat squadrons and additional helicopter, reconnaissance, and support squadrons as well as 12 transport squadrons. The navy has a total of 26 surface combatants and 16 submarines, including one aircraft carrier with another ordered from Russia. In addition, India has a one-million-strong paramilitary force of various categories under the control of the Ministry of Home Affairs.

With the recent streamlining of the military acquisition process, India continues to make some significant equipment purchases. Russia is by far the most important source of weapons for the Indian armed forces and this trend is likely to continue in the future. Major systems from Russia include co-production and transfer of technology of 140 Su 30 MkI and MiG 29 aircraft, T-90 tanks, and the "Smerch" multi-barrel rocket delivery system. Price negotiations for the aircraft aboard the aircraft carrier *Gorshkov* and cost of its repairs are in progress. Nine Kamov K-31 helicopters for the navy are likely to be received soon. The purchase price for 66 Hawk trainer jets from the United Kingdom has been finalized at about £1 billion (US$1.6 billion at £1 = US$1.60). Plans for the construction of six French Scorpene-class submarines at Mumbai's Mazagon docks are going ahead. The air force may be obtaining the Phalcon Airborne Warning and Control System (AWACS) from Israel in addition to the Searcher Unmanned Aerial Vehicles (UAVs). Finally, a contract was signed with the U.S. government for purchasing eight weapon-locating radars.

CONTRIBUTIONS TO REGIONAL AND GLOBAL SECURITY

India has continued its active role in regional security. Being a full dialogue partner of the Association of Southeast Asian Nations (ASEAN) and a member of the ASEAN Regional Forum (ARF), India has remained fully engaged with Southeast Asia in all its multilateral activities. India co-chaired along with Vietnam the ARF Inter-sessional Support Group on confidence-building measures and hosted the group's first meeting. India has also strengthened the Indian Ocean Rim Association for Regional Cooperation (IOR-ARC) and the Bangladesh-India-Myanmar-Sri Lanka-Thailand Economic Cooperation (BIMST-EC) grouping. A meeting of the foreign ministers of the BIMST-EC countries was held in Colombo in December 2002. Finally, India launched a Ganges-Mekong initiative to foster greater cooperation among the peoples inhabiting these two mighty river valleys. India is also actively engaged in the Conference on Interaction and Confidence-Building Measures in Asia (CICA) initiative launched by Kazakhstan in 1999, with the objective of promoting better relations among central Asian states. The long delayed 11th summit of the South Asian Association for Regional Cooperation (SAARC) was held at Kathmandu, Nepal, in January 2002. A Kathmandu Declaration was issued that outlined three main areas for the region: an economic agenda, poverty alleviation, and elimination of terrorism. The text of a draft treaty for establishing a South Asian Free Trade Area (SAFTA) by the end of 2002 has been delayed.

India is presently the fourth-largest contributor of troops to the UN peacekeeping operations. India has endorsed the Brahimi Commission Report on UN peacekeeping and commended the further strengthening of the UN Secretariat to help support operations in the field. India has in the past strongly supported cooperation between troop-contributing countries, the Security Council, and the Secretariat. A conference was convened, and a number of recommendations were made. A working group has been appointed to examine these and other peacekeeping issues. India has recently contributed 1,300 troops to the newly established United Nations Mission in Ethiopia and Eritrea (UNMEE). An Indian major general heads the UN Interim Force in Lebanon (UNIFIL).

India's policies on arms control and disarmament are guided by national security interests as well as its traditional policy of engaging the international community. India remains committed to nondiscriminatory and universal nuclear disarmament. Its preferred position is for the international community to conduct negotiations on a phased program for the complete elimination of nuclear weapons with a specified framework of time, including a nuclear weapons convention.

India supports efforts for negotiations on a universal, nondiscriminatory, and verifiable fissile material cutoff treaty that would prohibit the future production of fissile material for weapons purposes. India is committed to strengthening transparency in conventional arms and has regularly reported to the UN Conventional Arms Register since 1994. India has also been an original member of the Chemical Weapons Convention, completing the procedures for national implementation with the notification of the Chemical Weapons Convention Act on August 28, 2000. Over 60 inspections have been smoothly conducted in India by the Organization for the Prohibition of Chemical Weapons.

7 Indonesia

THE SECURITY ENVIRONMENT

Indonesia continues to experience an unstable and uncertain period in its political history following the 1998 collapse of the Suharto regime. The government of President Megawati Sukarnoputri has provided a veneer of political stability, but mainly relative to the chaotic regime of her predecessor, Abdurrahman Wahid. Indonesia remains beset by communal conflicts and separatist movements in Aceh and West Papua. The government's efforts to downplay the possibility that Indonesia harbored international terrorists were blown apart by the bombings in Bali on October 12, 2002, in which almost 200 Indonesians and foreign tourists were killed. Looking toward the external environment, Indonesians generally regard the Asia Pacific region as quite benign, with no problem directly threatening Indonesia's security or integrity. But the prospect of an American attack on Iraq, unless clearly supported by other Muslim nations, is a major source of anxiety for the regime and general public, who fear that Indonesia may be exploited by Islamic extremists hoping to ignite political unrest and to undermine government efforts to contain the radicals.

INTERNAL   Domestically for Indonesia the past year has been marked by two continuities—the gradual consolidation of democracy and continued ethnic and separatist conflict. There was also a discontinuity— the October terrorist bombings on Bali, which can be distinguished from other violence in the archipelago by their planning, intended targets, and impact on the Indonesian government and international relations.

Democratic Consolidation. The 10-day annual session of the People's Consultative Assembly (MPR, Majelis Permusyawaratan Rakyat) in August 2002 made some important decisions that helped institutionalize the new democratic system. The most fundamental change is that the president will be selected in 2004 by direct election instead of indirectly by MPR members themselves. This is seen as giving an advantage to Megawati, the best known politician with the strongest party organization. Also beginning in 2004, the military will no longer be allocated MPR seats. The military and police have already been largely phased out, holding only 38 of 700 seats in the MPR, but the termination of this political role has important symbolic value. Third, and in the face of a rise in political Islam, the MPR rejected a proposed constitutional amendment that would make Islamic law (the Shariah) state law for Muslims. That this last change occurred without major violence in the streets is a testament to the growth of stability in the Megawati period and to the continued commitment of the vast majority of Indonesians to the secular state.

For many Indonesians, however, the consolidation of democracy has been slow and has failed to bring with it the improvements that they had hoped for. Some blame the current president. During the past year, Megawati's leadership abilities, which have been questioned ever since she emerged in the political arena, came under more fire, including from within the ranks of her own political party, the PDI-P (Indonesian Democratic Party-Struggle). In particular, her judgment and vision have been criticized on several highly visible issues. In August, she endorsed the controversial Lt. General Sutijoso for reelection as governor of Jakarta. Since Sutijoso had headed the Jakarta military command at the time of Suharto's crackdown on Megawati's party in 1996, the move was widely regarded as politically expedient and even possibly related to the business ventures of the president's husband. Megawati had also appeared insensitive to the fate of hundreds of thousands of Indonesian workers who fled Malaysia in an immigration crackdown in August. Finally, she personally did not react with the vigor many Indonesians expected after the Bali bombings. There is as yet no strong public pressure on the president to step down, and she continues to enjoy the backing of the armed forces, but rival political aspirants, notably MPR Chair Amien Rais, have become increasingly vocal in their criticism.

One danger is that the president will increasingly align herself with the military, endangering the democratic and military reform processes.

Another rising danger is that public dissatisfaction may be vented not just at individual leaders but also at the democratic political system itself. This danger can come either from *reformasi* activists who believe that the changes in Indonesia have not addressed more fundamental social issues including poverty, income inequalities, and corruption or from authoritarian elements, including the military, seeking to exploit a new nostalgia for the more orderly Suharto period. Currently, such threats still appear remote since no influential leaders openly question the democratic system, but they are an inherent part of Indonesia's democratic transition.

Ethnic and Separatist Conflicts. Megawati's address to the August 2002 MPR session noted an easing of the "threat of national disintegration that has shadowed us in the past several years." The sectarian conflicts in Maluku and Poso (Central Sulawesi) have waned. At the time of the president's speech, however, there was little sign of improvement in Aceh and West Papua, hotbeds of separatism. The two provinces lie respectively at the far western and far eastern ends of the archipelago, and they have distinct cultural characteristics. Local populations have chafed under resource exploitation by outside interests, often without due regard for their customs and traditions with respect to resource use and ownership and often in collusion with government beneficiaries. The protection afforded such interests and facilities by Indonesian military and police adds to anti-government sentiments. The exploitive central rule and military brutality have left a legacy of bitterness that will take a long time to overcome even under the best circumstances.

Progress may have been made in the 26-year insurgency in Aceh that has cost an estimated 10,000 lives, mainly civilians. After months of negotiations, the government and leaders of the Free Aceh Movement (GAM, Gerakan Aceh Merdeka) signed a peace agreement in December 2002, brokered by the Henry Durant Center of Switzerland, that included an immediate ceasefire, a broad dialogue on Aceh's political future, and elections. The GAM is supposed to disarm over a seven-month period, while the central government will withdraw some of its 22,000 troops in the province. Like previous ceasefires in the Aceh conflict, the December agreement is a fragile one, and could easily be undone should either the government or the GAM believe that its interests were best served by renewing open struggle. The international monitors provided for in the agreement as well as a broad multilateral aid effort are considered crucial to the success of the peace agreement.

The Organisasi Papua Merdeka (OPM, Free Papua Movement)

conducts small-scale, sporadic guerrilla warfare in West Papua, sometimes spilling across the border into Papua New Guinea. However, agitation for independence has been largely peaceful and carried out under the auspices of the Presidium of the Papuan Council. The November 2001 murder by Indonesian soldiers of the chair of the Presidium, Theys Hiyo Eluay, escalated tensions in the province, and Laskar Jihad, a Java-based Islamic militia active in sectarian violence elsewhere in Indonesia, was said to be targeting the province, which has many more Christians than Muslims. As in Aceh, the Indonesian government has offered "special autonomy" over and above the local self-governance given to other provinces, but not yet on terms sufficiently attractive to a majority of the independence advocates. The most highly publicized incident of 2002 was the murder of three employees of the Freeport Copper and Gold Mine, said by some to have been carried out by the OPM and by others to have been carried out by local security forces to discredit the OPM. Coordinating Minister for Political and Security Affairs Susilo Bambang Yudhoyono says that securing peace in West Papua through international diplomacy and increased social justice in the province is a major priority for the government in 2003.

In post-Suharto Indonesia, sporadic incidents of violence have been common in the sectarian and separatist conflicts. Frequently they have involved local criminal interests. The October 12 Bali bombings were on a different order because they targeted tourists and Westerners, thus clearly giving the bombings an international dimension. The size and sophistication of the bombs made it apparent that outside technical and material assistance was involved.

The Bali Bombings. Prior to October, the Indonesian government was hesitant to crack down on local terrorists despite warnings and pleas from Singapore, Malaysia, Australia, and the United States. This was due in part to disbelief in the threat and in part to the political risks of appearing to carry out an "American" war on terrorism. After the bombings, the public mood shifted sharply toward condemning terrorism. The major Muslim organizations such as Muhammadiyan and Nahdatul Ulama denounced the bombings in the strongest terms as un-Islamic, and Laskar Jihad announced that it had previously decided to disband.

The Bali bombings horrified the Indonesian public and gave a sense of urgency to internal security efforts. New anti-terrorism legislation was passed on October 18, giving the Indonesian authorities the right to make preemptive arrests. The government detained Abu Bakar

Bashir, a co-founder of the Jemaah Islamiah (JI), a shadowy network of Islamic radicals operating in Indonesia, Malaysia, Singapore, and the southern Philippines. And, to the surprise of many observers, Indonesia's police, bolstered by outside cooperation, successfully apprehended some of the Bali perpetrators with considerable dispatch.

Police and other investigations are beginning to piece together a better picture of the terrorist threat in Indonesia, although many details remain murky. The JI appears to be the only organization with substantial international terrorist connections, with some of its members being veterans of operations in Afghanistan, the Philippines, and local conflicts within Indonesia. The group also appears to be quite small and decentralized.

The Bali bombings were another blow to Indonesia's fragile economy, which is continuing to make a very slow recovery from the crisis of 1997–1998. Prior to the bombings, the government had hoped for growth at about 3.5 percent for 2002, going up to 5 percent in 2003. These figures have had to be revised downward. The government plans to spend US$630 million on an emergency stimulus plan during 2003 to offset some of the damage. Oil prices and low interest rates have helped the Indonesian economy, but corruption, political uncertainty, lack of confidence in the legal system, labor unrest, and the failure to sell nationalized banks have all been negative factors.

EXTERNAL   Indonesia faces no conventional external threats. However, in terms of forces that impact on internal balances, there are multiple threats. One obvious source is international Islamist radicals such as al Qaeda, who threaten Indonesia by supplying inspiration and training to disillusioned young Indonesians. Other Indonesians perceive the West as a threat. In the aftermath of Bali, conspiracy theories abounded. According to one widely circulated story, the bombings were an elaborate plot hatched by the Central Intelligence Agency (CIA) to bring Indonesia firmly into the anti-terrorist coalition and to strengthen the internal role of the military and police. The quick passage of anti-terrorist legislation, which could be abused by the security forces, and efforts by the military to strengthen its local role gave further weight to this theory. Indonesian social reformers fear that renewed external support for the Indonesian police and the military from Western countries including the United States and Australia threatens democratic reform efforts.

Like others in Asia, Indonesians are concerned about the impact of the reemerging crisis in the Korean peninsula and the continued rivalry between mainland China and Taiwan. The latter affects Indonesia directly whenever high-ranking Taiwanese seek to visit the country. But the most serious international concern for Indonesia in 2003 comes from the potential impact of a conflict in Iraq. For many Indonesians, the war on terrorism is seen as an American war on Islam. Despite the tremendous sympathy Indonesians had for the victims of the September 11, 2001, attacks in the United States, the subsequent American action against the Taliban regime in Afghanistan was widely regarded as retaliatory and unjustified. Many in Indonesia fear that an American attack against Iraq, unless clearly supported by the United Nations or by other Muslim countries, would be very divisive internally and revive the failing fortunes of Islamic radicals.

DEFENSE POLICIES AND ISSUES

The evolving civil-military relationship and military reform remain the most important defense policy issues. The State Defense Act adopted in 2002 provides a greater role for the Parliament (DPR, Dewan Perwakilan Rakyat) in defense policies, specifically stipulating that any deployment for a military operation must have parliamentary approval. It also requires that the president's nominee for commander-in-chief of the armed forces be approved by Parliament and that the Ministry of Defense be headed by a civilian. Other recent reforms have included the progressive phasing out of military representation in the Parliament and the separation (in 1999) of the police from the military.

Many of these steps are important and meaningful symbols of the changing role of the defense establishment in Indonesian society. The reality, however, is that the actual processes of reform lag behind these symbolic measures. For example, the military continues to dominate the Ministry of Defense, in part simply because it will take some years before there is a sufficient pool of qualified civilians to take up these roles.

TERRITORIAL COMMAND   The Indonesian military is organized territorially, providing almost a parallel structure to civilian government throughout the country right down to the village level. This gives the military a continuing capacity to interfere with and even control much of society. Reform of the territorial command system has thus been a goal of both civilian and some military reformers. However, especially with the outbreak of communal and separatist violence, security problems in many remote areas, and the lack of trained police, the goal of achieving reform of the territorial structure will not be achieved easily. In fact, new regional commands have been created in Maluku and Aceh, and, following the Bali bombings, some in the military have argued that the territorial command actually needs to be strengthened in order to bring the armed forces closer to the people. Reformers are afraid that change in the territorial command system may either be deferred indefinitely or handled by the armed forces themselves rather than as part of a more comprehensive security and defense review by the civilian government.

A major conundrum for Indonesians is that the unrest and separatism in their country, combined with international terrorism, would seem to call for a stronger role than before for the armed forces, intelligence services, and the police. But a wide spectrum of Indonesians, including Muslims, democracy and human rights activists, and business people, continue to distrust the security and law forces because of their past record. They are much more inclined than foreign interests to see the military and police as a threat to civil liberties rather than as a solution to law and order problems, and they remain skeptical of early and easy reforms.

DEFENSE BUDGET   Military reform and budget issues are intertwined. Despite its numerous security problems, Indonesia's defense budget is estimated to be US$1 billion, only 1 percent of gross domestic product. As much as three-quarters of this amount goes into personnel costs. It is estimated that the government provides only about 25 percent–30 percent of the budget of the Indonesian National Military (TNI, Tentara Nasional Indonesia). To make up the gap, the military continues to find other sources of revenue, particularly in businesses. Some military enterprises are disguised as cooperatives and foundations, while others operate quite openly as commercial enterprises. The military enterprises create political and economic links between the military and the political and business communities that impede or negate accountability and control. Raising funds becomes a central interest of the military to the detriment of professional military activities. The necessity of raising revenue also helps explain the continued value to the military of the territorial command system. This is another long-term problem plaguing Indonesia's security system, and one in which very little practical progress has been made thus far in the post-Suharto reform era.

Contributions to Regional and Global Security

The main contribution that Indonesia can make to regional and global security comes from strengthening Indonesia as a well-governed state. An Indonesia that is weak or riddled with corruption obviously becomes a haven for pirates, human and drug traffickers, and terrorists. One positive development flowing from the Bali bombings has been much more active and serious cooperation between Indonesian intelligence and police services and their international counterparts, including in Australia and the United States as well as Indonesia's Southeast Asian neighbors. This intensified collaboration has contributed to disrupting the JI network in Southeast Asia and preventing other terrorist incidents. As is often emphasized, however, security issues such as terrorism must be addressed comprehensively. The bigger and longer-term challenges for Indonesia and its international friends remain the strengthening of democratic civilian governance of the country and restarting the economy.

Despite its absorption with internal issues in recent years, Indonesia continues to be active in the Association of Southeast Asian Nations (ASEAN), the ASEAN Regional Forum (ARF), the Asia-Pacific Economic Cooperation (APEC) forum, the Asia-Europe Meeting (ASEM), and the emerging ASEAN + 3 (China, Japan, and South Korea) process, including the ongoing efforts by these multilateral arrangements to address international terrorism.

8 Japan

The Security Environment

Japan faces yet another year of difficult challenges both at home and abroad. On the domestic front, the economy remains afflicted by prolonged stagnation and deflation. Prime Minister Koizumi Jun'ichirō's ability to set strong policy leadership is hamstrung by powerful vested interests entrenched in the political and bureaucratic systems. On the foreign policy front, North Korea presents the most difficult continuing challenge for Japan, while in 2003, Japan is also grappling with its Iraqi policy. While Japan appeared to make headway toward normalizing its relations with Pyongyang when Koizumi visited there in September 2002, controversy over the fate of Japanese abducted by the North Korean government, North Korea's confession that it is pursuing a nuclear weapons program, and North Korea's announced determination to restart the reactors frozen by the 1994 Agreed Framework aroused profound concern in Japan and elsewhere. Iraq raises difficult questions for Japan regarding balances between its alliance relationship with the United States, international responsibilities more generally, its own judgments regarding the best approach to Iraq's defiance of UN inspections, and compliance with its domestic constitutional and political constraints.

INTERNAL   Prime Minister Koizumi remains personally quite popular and faces no immediate challenge to his leadership. In January 2002, he weathered a storm after he fired controversial, outspoken, and popular Minister of Foreign Affairs Tanaka Makiko after damaging strife between her and officials in the Ministry of Foreign Affairs. In the wake of this and political scandals involving influential Liberal Democratic Party (LDP) members Katō Kōichi and Suzuki Muneo, Koizumi's approval ratings fell from their 70 percent–80 percent levels in 2001 to the 40 percent–50 percent level. His popularity had a second boost after his surprise visit to North Korea in September, but not to the previous levels. Despite these setbacks and increased grumbling from LDP members about Koizumi's economic policies and leadership style, no credible alternative to the prime minister seems apparent, either from within his party or from the fractious opposition parties.

The key challenge for Koizumi is how to convert his personal popularity into policy effectiveness, particularly since he lacks a strong political base within the ruling party. The weakness of policy effectiveness is most evident in the economic policy sphere, where Koizumi has pledged to accelerate structural reforms to jumpstart the economy amid deflationary pressures and deepening recession. The banking system, burdened by enormous amounts of nonperforming loans (NPLs), is seen as the major impediment to revival because high levels of NPLs discourage new lending and help keep "zombie" firms in business. But pledges by the government to get tough with the banks, most notably in October 2002 after the appointment of Takenaka Heizō as economics and financial services minister, have consistently run up against entrenched political and economic interests. In the process, compromises have been made vitiating the reforms or implementation has not matched government rhetoric. Cumbersome decision-making processes; collusive relations among politicians, bureaucrats, and big business; and a continuing fondness for pork-barrel politics all inhibit serious and rapid policy reforms. The prime minister's critics argue that he has cut out important elements from his own party that should be brought into a consensus-building process, thus aggravating opposition to his policies.

EXTERNAL   While the growth of Chinese power is frequently regarded as the biggest structural shift in Asian and perhaps global international relations, North Korea represents Japan's most immediate and serious foreign and security policy challenge. Koizumi seized the initiative by visiting Pyongyang on September 17, 2002, and signing a Pyongyang Declaration with Kim Jong Il. This paved the way for resumption of the normalization talks that had been stalled since October 2000. Kim seemed anxious for rapprochement, admitting and apologizing for kidnappings of Japanese nationals in the 1970s and 1980s and for spy ships' intrusions into Japanese waters. This openness backfired for Pyongyang, however, as the Japanese people were outraged by the shocking revelation that eight of the dozen admitted Japanese abductees had died, while only five abductees were subsequently allowed to return to Japan.

North Korean diplomacy was further complicated in October by Washington's revelation that Pyongyang had also admitted to an ongoing secret uranium enrichment program in violation of the 1994 Agreed Framework between the United States and North Korea. In the face of North Korea's violation of its international agreements, which also include agreements to which Japan is a party such as the Nonproliferation Treaty (NPT) and the Japan-North Korea Pyongyang Declaration as well as North Korea's inspection agreement with the International Atomic Energy Agency (IAEA), Tokyo decided against concluding its normalization talks and extending economic aid unless Pyongyang abandons its nuclear weapons program and resolves the abduction issues. The North Korean government has so far shown no remorse, claiming that its nuclear aspirations were justified by Washington's aggressiveness; it has disabled IAEA monitoring equipment and taken steps to restart frozen reactors. The Japanese government hopes to defuse the rapidly escalating crisis in solidarity with the United States, South Korea, China, Russia, and the UN agencies.

While maintaining the alliance with the United States as the lynchpin of Japan's security policy, Tokyo is seeking to expand its own interests and relationships in East Asia. In January 2002 in Singapore, Koizumi proposed the creation of a new community "that acts together and advances together" with the Association of Southeast Asian Nations (ASEAN), Japan, China, South Korea, Australia, and New Zealand as its core members. Economically the proposal was aimed at the deepening of regional economic cooperation manifest in the intensifying patterns of trade and investment and the development of regional institutions such as the ASEAN + 3 (China, Japan, and South Korea) forum. But the proposal also had an important political base in the common desire for political stability in the region.

Japan's relations with China and South Korea are maturing, despite occasional problems. China looms large in Japan's economic activities and its long-term strategy as Japan's largest aid recipient, its second-largest trade partner, and, increasingly, its production base. Tokyo has actively been engaged in policy consultations with Seoul vis-à-vis North Korea, together with the United States. The huge success of the 2002

World Cup soccer competition jointly hosted by Japan and South Korea improved the public perceptions of each country in the other. The North Korean crisis and bilateral economic opportunities provide a basis for trying to give new momentum to the normalization of Japan's relations with Russia, stalled by the territorial dispute over the Northern Territories. Recognizing Russia's inability to move on a territorial settlement, Koizumi, during his visit to Moscow in January 2003, proposed a comprehensive approach designed to strengthen the bilateral relationship at all levels, including economic cooperation, security policy consultations, and cultural and human exchanges. In particular, the action plan, signed by Koizumi and Russian President Vladimir Putin, noted that the two countries encourage joint development of oil and natural gas resources in Siberia, which would involve two ambitious plans: one to construct an oil pipeline that would bring 1 million barrels of oil a day from western Siberia to Nakhodka, and another to develop huge oil and gas deposits off the coast of Sakhalin Island. These plans, if materialized, could significantly reduce Tokyo's dependence on oil from the Middle East from 83 percent to 65 percent.

Japan's relationship with Australia has long been characterized by economic complementarity especially in trade and investment. In May 2002, Koizumi suggested that the two governments construct a "creative partnership . . . that would enhance exchanges on political and security issues, strengthen economic ties and intensify cooperation, and share experiences on educational, social, scientific, technological and other matters." As core members of the "community" proposed by Koizumi in Singapore, Japan and Australia would not only strengthen their economic partnership but also expand their joint efforts for regional security in areas such as peacekeeping, anti-terrorist measures, and anti-piracy operations.

DEFENSE POLICIES AND ISSUES

DEFENSE PLANNING   In 2003, Japan will be in the third year of its 2001–2005 Mid-Term Defense Program (MTDP) (see *Asia Pacific Security Outlook 2001*). In light of the changing security environment, defense policy and needs are under review. The Council on the Modality of Defense Capability, set up in September 2001 and headed by the defense minister, is conducting studies on future defense capabilities, paying particular attention to advancement in science and technology, the situation on the Korean peninsula, and demographic and economic conditions.

While modernizing defense capability in line with the MTDP, the Defense Agency has begun planning for operational integration of the Ground, Maritime and Air Self-Defense Forces (SDF). The operations of the SDF, including disaster relief operations and UN peacekeeping, are currently conducted separately by the three services under orders from the defense minister. The new policy under consideration will require the chairman of the Joint Staff Council (JSC) to directly command elements of the three services so that they can perform their duties promptly and effectively. To this end, a new organization providing support for the JSC chairman will be established.

Japanese defense policymakers have long recognized the necessity for establishing a legal framework for mobilizing the SDF in the event of an emergency, yet most legislators, including those of the LDP, have shunned the issue of emergency legislation in fear of public backlash. The government finally is trying to address this issue, although the outlook is not good. In April 2002, for the first time since the end of World War II, three defense bills related to emergency legislation were drawn up and submitted to the Diet. The proposed legislation includes an emergency contingency bill to deal with direct military attacks on the nation; an amendment to the SDF Law that would enable SDF personnel to engage in operations effectively in a military emergency; and a bill to amend the Security Council Establishment Law so as to grant the council greater power to deal with an emergency.

Critics argue that the bills are flawed in some important respects. First, under the legislation, the SDF would be mobilized not only in the event of an armed attack against Japan but also when an armed attack is either "imminent" or "anticipated," without providing clear criteria for judging either of these attack conditions. Second, the bills fail to incorporate more likely types of security threats such as terrorist attacks and sea incursions by armed vessels. Third, the legislation lacks provisions for protecting lives and assets of the people, including measures for evacuations, recovery of damages, and for ensuring transportation, communication, and other public facilities. It only suggests that additional legislation on these matters will be required within two years. Fourth, the legislation fails to specify the ways in which a Japanese response to a military emergency would be linked up with U.S. action under the bilateral defense cooperation guidelines that apply to regional contingencies. Given the opposition's objections to the proposed legislation and the lack of public consensus on emergency legislation, the enactment of the legislation seems politically difficult.

COLLECTIVE SECURITY   Since the September 11, 2001, terrorist attacks in the United States, Tokyo has strongly supported and assisted the U.S.-led coalition in the war against terrorism. With the passage in October 2001 of the Anti-Terrorism Special Measures Law, the role of Japan's SDF has significantly expanded: SDF vessels were sent to the Indian Ocean to provide supplies of fuel to U.S. and U.K. naval ships there; and SDF aircraft are engaged in transportation support for U.S. forces. These deployments have been reauthorized at six-month intervals, and logistic support increasingly given to other forces in the region.

Throughout the year, the Japanese policy community has been concerned about how to position itself with respect to possible U.S. military action against Iraq. On the one hand, Japan does not want to annoy an important ally, one reason that the Japanese government has been less vocal than Germany, China, Russia, or France in voicing reservations to U.S. policy, although many in Tokyo have reservations. The government has also been anxious to avoid a repeat of its tardiness in 1991 in the Gulf War, to which it contributed substantial financial assistance but so late that it got virtually no credit for its action. On the other hand, Tokyo desires a clear mandate for military action from the United Nations and a compelling rationale from the United States.

In mid-December, the government dispatched an Aegis-equipped destroyer to the Indian Ocean in support of the war on terrorism. Although made in the context of the war on terrorism, the deployment of the Aegis destroyer is regarded as indirect support for U.S. action in Iraq by freeing up U.S. ships to position themselves farther westward as there is no operations development in Afghanistan that would require enhanced Japanese support. The Japanese government has also indicated it can provide humanitarian and post-conflict reconstruction assistance to Iraq.

DEFENSE SPENDING AND PERSONNEL   Japan's defense budget for fiscal 2002 was ¥4,939.5 billion (US$39.5 billion at US$1 = ¥125), an almost zero percent increase over the previous year's budget. The ratio of defense spending to gross national product was projected to be 0.995 percent in 2002. Of the budget, 45.1 percent was allocated to personnel and provisions, 18.6 percent to equipment and materiels, 18.4 percent to operational maintenance (including education and training), 10.5 percent to base security and support for U.S. forces in Japan, 3.2 percent to base and facilities maintenance, and 2.6 percent to research and development. In addition, the government earmarked ¥16.5 billion (US$132 million) as expenses for the Japan-U.S. Special Action Committee on Okinawa (SACO). These defense expenditure figures do not include spending on the coast guard or pensions, and therefore are not comparable to North Atlantic Treaty Organization (NATO) measures of defense effort.

The SDF had 239,839 active duty personnel as of March 2002. The Ground Self-Defense Force (GSDF) has 148,197 members, the Maritime Self-Defense Force (MSDF) has 44,404 members, the Air Self-Defense Force (ASDF) has 45,582 members, and the Joint Staff Council has 1,656 members. Efforts to recruit SDF personnel have been more successful in recent years, primarily due to the continuing economic stagnation and bleak job market. In the medium to long term, however, recruitment will become more difficult as the population of males between the ages of 18 and 26, which peaked in 1994, continues to dwindle.

PROCUREMENT   Japan's current defense buildup has been promoted in line with the MTDP. Major procurements undertaken in fiscal year 2002 or initiated in that year include the following.

- For the GSDF: 18 Type-90 tanks, one Type-89 armored combat vehicle, 149 light armored mobile vehicles, 15 Type-96 wheeled armored vehicles, seven Type-99 15 mm self-propelled new howitzers, three multiple launch rocket systems (MLRS), two multipurpose helicopters (UH-60JA), two transport helicopters (CH-47JA), two combat helicopters (AH-64D), two OH-1 helicopters, two sets of Type-96 multi-purpose missile systems, 13 sets of Type-93 short-range surface-to-air missiles, 39 sets of Type-91 portable surface-to-air missiles, and 242 sets of Type-01 light anti-tank guided missiles.
- For the MSDF: one 7,700-ton-class destroyer, one 2,700-ton-class submarine, one 510-ton-class minesweeper, seven patrol helicopters (SH-60K), and one rescue amphibian (US-1A).
- For the ASDF: eight fighter-support aircraft (F-2), two transport helicopters (CH-47J), one Boeing 767 tanker (aerial refueling) aircraft, one rescue helicopter (UH-60J), and two groups of the improved surface-to-air missiles (Patriot).

Among these, the most significant is the purchase of Japan's first airborne refueling airplane (Boeing 767). The cost of the refueling airplane will be paid for over five years starting in fiscal 2002, and the actual deployment of the aircraft is expected around fiscal 2006. The acquisition of aerial refueling capability would expand the scope of operations of the SDF, contributing to collective security operations with the United States and international peacekeeping and disaster relief activities. This, however, can be seen as Japan's acquisition of limited power-projection capability, thus potentially provocative to Japan's neighbors. The procurement for fiscal 2002 also features equipment to counter biological and other types of guerrilla attacks and for creation of a more advanced telecommunications network in the Defense Agency headquarters and the SDF.

CONTRIBUTIONS TO REGIONAL AND GLOBAL SECURITY

MILITARY AND DIPLOMATIC CONTRIBUTIONS   The Japan-U.S. alliance serves not only as a major pillar of Japan's security policy but also as a stabilizing factor in peace and stability in the Asia Pacific region. With the U.S.-Japan alliance as the basis of its external security policy, Japan is actively engaged in regional institutions such as the Asia-Pacific Economic Cooperation (APEC) forum, the ASEAN Regional Forum (ARF), the ASEAN + 3 process, and the Asia-Europe Meeting (ASEM). Tokyo is also a strong supporter of global institutions such as the United Nations and the World Trade Organization (WTO), as well as global arms control and non-proliferation regimes such as the Comprehensive Test Ban Treaty (CTBT) and the NPT.

Aside from the logistical support in the Indian Ocean, Japan is assisting in the global war against terrorism in other ways. It sent its emergency Terrorism Response Team of police experts to Bali after the bombings there in October 2002 (in which two Japanese had lost their lives), and it is looking to cooperate with Australia, Singapore, and the Association of Southeast Asian Nations (ASEAN) group as a whole on counter-terrorist activities.

ECONOMIC CONTRIBUTIONS   Official Development Assistance (ODA) is one of the most valuable instruments of Japan's foreign policy, helping to compensate for Japan's limited direct-security contributions. From 1991 through 2000, Japan was the world's largest aid donor to developing countries. However, because of its fiscal constraints, there has been a substantial decline in ODA. In 2001, Japan provided US$9.68 billion in ODA, down 28.4 percent from the previous year, but still making Japan the world's second-largest aid donor. It is expected that there will be further cutbacks in Tokyo's ODA budgets in future years.

Japan's ODA is becoming more and more controversial for several reasons—the tight fiscal situation, the lack of transparency in ODA projects, and the granting of assistance to countries where the aid might be misused or policies pursued inimical to good governance. In 2001, as a result of such criticisms, Tokyo altered its ODA policy toward China. The new policy requires that official loans be pledged on a project-by-project basis each year instead of making multiyear pledges. This resulted in a 25 percent cut in aid pledged to China in fiscal 2001. A final report prepared by the foreign minister's advisory committee on ODA was submitted in March 2002, calling for more focused, effective, and publicly accountable ODA policies, including incorporating "development education" into the school curriculum, the formulation of country-specific aid programs, collaboration with nongovernmental organizations, and the establishment of a permanent Board on Comprehensive ODA Strategy. The 2001 ODA white paper, released in May 2002, emphasizes that building partnerships with NGOs, enhanced transparency of aid projects, and citizen participation are increasingly important, given the growing public criticism of ODA.

UN PEACEKEEPING AND HUMANITARIAN ASSISTANCE   On the request of the United Nations, the SDF engineering battalion (680 personnel) participated in the UN Transitional Administration in East Timor (UNTAET) and the subsequent UN Mission of Support in East Timor (UNMISET). This was the largest deployment of its type, exceeding that of the SDF contingent dispatched to Cambodia in 1992–1993. Additionally, ten SDF personnel were in East Timor as UNTAET and UNMISET military section headquarters staff. Japan continues to take part in the UN Disengagement Observer Force in the Golan Heights.

9 Republic of Korea

THE SECURITY ENVIRONMENT

INTERNAL   Many Koreans, who characterize each year according to one of the 12 animals of Chinese astrology, expected 2002—the year of the galloping horse, or Yi Jing, which comes every 60 years—to bring political chaos, revolt, and even war. They were not disappointed. Political developments last year occurred at a "galloping speed," especially toward the end of the year. The Korean peninsula entered 2003 as an unexpected crisis erupted over North Korea's efforts to develop nuclear weapons, a concern supposedly resolved almost a decade ago. The South began a leadership transition as Roh Moo Hyun, of Kim Dae Jung's Millennium Democratic Party, won a narrow, unpredictable victory in the December 2002 elections. The two main candidates were distinguished by their different approaches on the North Korea nuclear issue, with Roh strongly committed to following Kim's "Sunshine Policy" of engagement with North Korea.

Whereas Kim's political power base was in his home region in the southwest, Roh's support appeared to be less regional and more generational in orientation. He particularly appealed to the more youthful electorate, apparently winning as much as 60 percent of voters who have had no first-hand experience of the extreme poverty of the 1950s and 1960s or the Korean War. A liberal labor lawyer, Roh has no experience in international affairs. He has questioned the usefulness of American forces in Korea, a position he disavows today. Like Kim, he must contend with an opposition party majority in the National Assembly.

Aside from the North Korea problem, discussed below, the economy deeply concerns ordinary Koreans and presents a major challenge for the new administration in 2003. In 2002, the South's economy looked quite healthy and was widely praised abroad for the government's relatively successful reforms in response to the 1997–1998 Asian economic crisis. At 6.3 percent in 2002, South Korea had the world's third-highest gross domestic product growth rates after China and Vietnam. Compared to many of its neighbors, South Korea enjoyed low unemployment, stable economic policies, and political stability. The 2003 economic outlook is less robust. Export growth has slowed, and household loans are almost US$25,000 per family. The downward spiral of the Korea Composite Stock Price Index reached the psychological threshold level of 600 and threatens to unleash a raft of household bankruptcies. At the same time, low interest rates have caused a recent bubble in the real estate market and cause the high level of household debts. The government is hesitant to raise interest rates at a time of slow growth. It is hoping for renewed trade with the United States and Europe, and is encouraged by the growing economic ties with China, both a partner and potential competitor in South Korean industries.

EXTERNAL   The inclusion of North Korea as part of U.S. President George W. Bush's "axis of evil" connected the North to the volatile Middle East and suggested that the Korean peninsula will remain a region of conflict. Ironically, however, South Koreans themselves are much less worried about the possibility of a terrorist attack on their own soil from either North Korea or the Middle East. The World Cup and the Asian Games were well hosted by the Koreans with no threat of terrorism. The top concern among Koreans, however, is the aftermath or side-effect of an imminent U.S. war against terrorism in the Middle East and the possibility that North Korea would become the next target after Iraq. The October 2002 admission by North Korea of a nuclear program greatly reinforces these worries among Koreans.

The North Korea situation remains South Korea's main external security concern, followed by the impact that U.S. actions in the Middle East may have on the Korean peninsula. Public opinion polls, however, show that relatively few South Koreans, particularly younger ones, see the North as a direct military threat. In fact, Japanese and Americans often appear to be more concerned with North Korea's conventional military, missile, and potential nuclear capabilities than South Koreans. South Koreans have lived with the North Korean threat for over five decades, and during this time the North has gone from being the more economically and militarily powerful state in the peninsula to becoming an economic disaster zone. The North is now widely perceived in the South as highly vulnerable and defensive, not an aggressive threat unless acting out of desperation. Increasingly, South Koreans regard the threat from the North as less one of military aggression than one of indirect and unintended consequences of its relations with outside powers, particularly the United States.

The immediate concern is the North Korean reaction to the stoppage of U.S. fuel shipments under the 1994 Agreed Framework. Pyongyang removed the International Atomic Energy Agency (IAEA) seals and cameras from its reprocessing facilities and expelled international monitors. This was followed by the North's announcement that it would restart its reactor plants, withdraw from the Nonproliferation Treaty (NPT), begin new missile tests, and withdraw from the armistice agreement. Coming in rapid succession, these steps created a full-blown crisis on the Korean peninsula reminiscent of North Korea's proposed withdrawal from the NPT in 1993–1994.

Despite the different views within South Korea on how the North should be approached, there is a wide national consensus on some basic features: any Korean war would have unacceptable costs, North Korea should be helped in its development by encouraging incremental change within the state, and both South and North should work to end the division of the peninsula. This consensus accounts for the continuity in South Korean policy toward the North, despite the periodic changes in South Korean leadership. Because of the tremendous price that war would have for the Korean people, South Koreans generally favor a non-provocative approach toward Pyongyang.

The high point of South Korean hopes for a new beginning in South-North relations came with the June 2000 summit meeting in Pyongyang. Despite talk of linking railways, family visits, and a return trip by Kim Jong Il for a second summit in Seoul, the inter-Korean dialogue slowed down in the months after the summit. There is little evidence that Kim Jong Il is seriously prepared to come to Seoul. Kim Dae Jung doggedly pursued his trademark Sunshine Policy approach, but the North-South relationship turned increasingly sour after President Bush took office. While the new American administration often gave mixed signals, Bush from the start expressed skepticism toward the Sunshine Policy approach, and Pyongyong used this as a rationale for its cautionary response to the inter-Korean projects.

Ironically, Bush's January 2002 reference to North Korea as a member of an axis of evil seemed to spark new movement on the Korean peninsula. Outcries in South Korea against Bush's controversial remarks calmed down during the U.S.–South Korea summit in Seoul in February. Seoul helped engineer Pyongyang's acceptance of a visit by a U.S. special envoy, which was later postponed due to a naval clash in June between North and South Korea along the maritime border in the West Sea (Yellow Sea).

In late July, North Korea expressed regret about the naval battle and suggested holding an inter-Korean ministerial-level meeting between the two Koreas. Pyongyang also sent a delegation to the ASEAN Regional Forum (ARF) meeting where North Korean Foreign Minister Paek Nam Sun briefly chatted with U.S. Secretary of State Colin Powell. During the inter-Korean talks, North Korea agreed to implement previous agreements. Cross-border railroad and highway construction projects were put back on the agenda, more land mines were to be eliminated, and new emergency hot lines were proposed between the two states. A possible defense ministers' meeting and institutionalized family reunions were also discussed. In September, North Korea hosted Japanese Prime Minister Koizumi Jun'ichirō, at which time Kim Jong Il admitted that his country had abducted Japanese citizens over the past several decades and agreed to send five survivors to Japan for family visits.

In another set of positive developments, North Korea undertook sweeping market-oriented reforms, declaring it would revamp the commodities' pricing system and introduce performance-based pay from July 1, 2002. It also announced that it would promote foreign direct investment by designating special administrative zones in Shinuiju and Gaesung. Despite international skepticism about whether the projects would materialize, Kim Jong Il made some irreversible economic decisions. These political and economic developments gave South Koreans hope that new reforms would emerge from Pyongyang that would benefit South-North relations. These hopes were threatened when Americans reported in October that the North Koreans had admitted to a uranium enrichment program in violation of the U.S.–North Korea 1994 Agreed Framework.

Concerning the inter-Korean relationship, the U.S.–South Korea alliance and U.S.–North Korea relations are so closely intertwined that they cannot be considered in isolation from each other. Each is a key factor in determining security and prosperity in Northeast Asia. Part of the security dilemma for South Koreans is that their country has so little direct control over or even influence on the dynamics of U.S.–North Korea relations, which so seriously affect their own security. South Korea, for example, was not a party of the 1994 Framework Agreement (although it ended up paying much of the bill for the agreement). Also, South Korea's government could not substantially influence the hard-line approach adopted by Bush after he took office in 2001. Although the United States concedes that South Korea should take the lead on policy toward the North, in the eyes of the Korean leadership, the United States has failed to support South Korea's preferred policy approach.

When South Korean hopes were dashed again at the end of 2002, Korean frustration was vented publicly against the U.S. approach. Many blamed the United States for provoking the crisis, citing the lack of interest on the part of the Bush administration in continuing the more forthcoming dialogue of the previous administration. Bush's "axis of evil" speech, the possible misinterpretation of the North Korean "admission" of a nuclear program, and the adamant refusal of the United States for weeks after October 2002 to consider further discussions until Pyongyang abandoned its nuclear programs also prompted South Korean concerns. On the other side, South Korean critics of the North pointed out that the North Koreans had apparently started the uranium enrichment program in violation of the Framework Agreement well before Bush was even elected and that Pyongyang continued to take steps to provoke a crisis even as Washington was describing the confrontation as diplomatic rather than military in nature. The South Korean government faces simultaneously challenges of wanting to stop the North Korean nuclear program, to maintain a robust alliance with the United States, and to continue the dialogue approach with the North.

The relationship with the United States remains a fundamental element of South Korean defense and foreign policy, but it has become increasingly controversial. In addition to differences in the dominant approaches by their governments toward the North, a series of incidents relating to U.S. bases in South Korea and the status of U.S. forces in the country contribute to these tensions. The November 2002 judgment by a U.S. military court that the drivers of a military vehicle that had killed two South Korean teenage girls were not criminally negligent in the accident triggered large demonstrations in Seoul during which American flags were burned. In the view of many commentators, the demonstrations helped Roh Moo Hyun to his election victory, since he was clearly more critical of the United States than conservative rival Lee Hoi

Chang. To make the foreign presence more acceptable, Roh is likely to ask for further review of the Status of Forces Agreement (SOFA) and realignment of the bases to remove U.S. forces from central Seoul and reduce their size. But these changes may not help deal with the more general problem in the alliance, which is that South Koreans often feel their interests are slighted in Washington.

In South Korea, the new North Korean crisis pushed to the background concerns about the other international crisis directed at Iraq over weapons of mass destruction. Many South Koreans believe that the United States, which is concentrating on Iraq, is buying time with its diplomacy in North Korea. But after Iraq, they worry that North Korea may become a new U.S. target for either economic sanctions or a preemptive strike. Both scenarios would inevitably escalate tensions, with a possibility of massive conflict on the Korean peninsula.

Over the longer term, the dilemma facing Seoul is how to strengthen its influence on inter-Korean issues. In this respect, Seoul has increasingly looked to its neighbors, Japan, China, and Russia, for support. All three countries have deep stakes in the Korean peninsula. Although each has its own approach, all generally share the current Seoul government's policy preferences—no tolerance of nuclear weapons but a cautious approach to any kind of sanctions. In the wake of the U.S.–North Korean stalemate, the South Korean government closely consulted with all three neighbors, especially China, in the hopes of putting pressure on both Pyongyang and Washington so as to return conditions to the status quo ante.

Relations with China and Japan have dimensions beyond the North Korean issue. Since the normalization between the two Koreas in 1992, their economic relationship has grown rapidly. In 2002, China (including Hong Kong) surpassed the United States by becoming South Korea's top export market, totaling US$22.9 billion. South Korea's exports to China rose at an average annual rate of 23.8 percent in the same year. Investment is also growing rapidly in Shandong province, Tianjin, and Liaoning province—key destinations for South Korean investment in China. The total amount of South Korean investment in China is expected to reach about US$1.5 billion in 2002.

Relations with Japan improved with the successful holding of the 2002 World Cup games. Surveys show that younger Koreans, those largely supporting Roh, have fewer negative images of Japan than the older generation. For this reason, the cultural and psychological aspects of Korean-Japanese relations are likely to be normalized, although symbolic events, like the Yasukuni Shrine visits of the Japanese prime minister, remain problems for the future.

DEFENSE POLICIES AND ISSUES

From South Korea's total budget of 111.7 trillion won (US$93.28 billion at US$1 = 1,197.5 won) for 2003, 17.4 trillion won (US$14.53 billion) was earmarked for the defense budget, an increase of 6.4 percent over 2002. The Ministry of National Defense planned the purchase of F-15Ks, upgrades of combat capability, and improvement of base facilities. Additional procurements for 2003 cost 308.4 billion won (US$257.54 million) and include portable anti-aircraft missiles, high-speed patrol boats, combat hovercraft, and a presidential helicopter.

The South Korean defense budget is about 2.7 percent of gross domestic product and 15.5 percent of government outlays. For the last five years, the average growth of the defense budget has been 4.8 percent, which is less than half of the growth rate for the total government budget of 10.6 percent. Since the world average for defense outlay is about 4 percent of GDP, South Korea's defense budget is not high by international standards. Other countries with imminent security threats, such as Israel and Pakistan, have defense budgets around 8 percent, three times higher than that of South Korea. South Korea is focusing on building an advanced military force based on information and technology as only one way to simultaneously prepare against threats from North Korea and other unspecified threats in the future. It is not difficult to imagine that a unified Korea in the new century will most likely face potential pressure from surrounding big powers. Awareness of shifting geopolitics remains a priority to South Korea's security planners. Aside from this, South Korea is improving compensation and living conditions for on-duty servicemen and retired personnel. To pay for this over the longer term, the Defense Ministry's 2002 policy review calls for increasing the defense budget to more than 3 percent of GDP by 2015.

CONTRIBUTIONS TO REGIONAL AND GLOBAL SECURITY

South Korea contributes to regional and global security through its efforts to maintain peace on the Korean peninsula and by participating in UN peacekeeping, building regional and global institutions, promoting liberalized trade bilaterally and multilaterally, and contributing to development assistance.

A centerpiece of South Korea's efforts toward peace is the promotion of an East Asian community as a complement to inter-regional cooperation through institutions such as the Asia-Europe Meeting (ASEM) and the Asia-Pacific Economic Cooperation (APEC) forum. The South Korean government has found that regional organizations such as the ASEAN Regional Forum are good arenas to engage North Korea. Under Kim Dae Jung, the South Korean government has sought to bring North Korea into such organizations so that it will become a more cooperative member of international and regional communities. The South is also using ASEM, APEC, and other institutions for seeking understanding and cooperation from international society on peaceful means of changing North Korea, thereby improving the security situation on the Korean peninsula.

South Korea has successfully carried out its term of presidency of the UN General Assembly, laying the groundwork to become a member of the UN Economic and Social Council (ECOSOC) for 2004–2006 and a non-permanent member of the UN Security Council in the year 2007–2008. The country has supported UN peacekeeping since 1993 when South Korea dispatched an engineer battalion to Somalia. In the past decade, some 4,000 South Korean peacekeepers have been deployed to seven different locations including East Timor, Angola, and the western Sahara. As of June 2002, 475 South Korean soldiers were abroad on peacekeeping missions in five different regions of conflict. In 2002, the military sent nine officers to the UN Military Observer Group in India and Pakistan (UNMOGIP) and five to the UN Observer Mission in Georgia (UNOMIG). South Korean officers on those missions served under the supervision of local commanders and conducted such activities as monitoring ceasefires, patrolling, inspection, report, and arbitration.

On the economic side, South Korea is actively participating in the Doha Development Agenda negotiations of the World Trade Organization (WTO). It is being pressured by the international community to open its markets in telecommunications, education, and legal and medical fields and to lower trade restrictions in the fields of accounting, distribution, construction, and finance. A free trade agreement with Chile has just been signed, a similar accord with Japan is being studied, and others have been proposed. The government is establishing special economic zones along the coastal areas such as in Inchon, Busan, and Kwangyang to intensify efforts to support exports and attract foreign investment.

South Korea is gradually increasing its Official Development Assistance (ODA) and strengthening cooperation in the information and technology fields to help developing countries overcome the digital divide. South Korea allocates 0.08 percent of its GDP to overseas development aid, still far less than other members of the Organization for Economic Co-operation and Development (OECD). The Association of Southeast Asian Nations (ASEAN) is a major focus of South Korean ODA efforts. South Korea's Economic Development Cooperation Fund provides loans and development expertise to Vietnam, Indonesia, and the Philippines, while the Korea International Cooperation Agency assists Myanmar, Cambodia, and Laos.

10 Malaysia

THE SECURITY ENVIRONMENT

Despite heightened concerns about terrorism, brought closer to home by the bombings in Bali in October 2002, Malaysians are generally optimistic about their own security environment in 2003. They enter the year, however, with deep concern that U.S. and U.K. approaches to terrorism, which emphasize military dimensions but fail to give serious attention to the root causes, will undermine Malaysia's counter-terrorist efforts domestically, regionally, and globally and worsen the problem of terrorism. The deepening confrontation over Iraq threatens to further inflame global Western-Muslim tensions, placing Malaysia, which has strong connections to both worlds, in a particularly challenging position. Malaysia is also facing a change of leadership. After 21 years, Prime Minister Mahathir bin Mohammed has announced his intention to step down toward the end of 2003, paving the way for his appointed successor, Abdullah Haji Ahmad Badawi, more affectionately known as Pak Lah.

INTERNAL Domestically, Malaysia continues to combat militancy and terrorism. It has so far arrested approximately 70 suspects connected to the Kumpulan Militan Malaysia (KMM) and Jemaah Islamiah (JI) under the Internal Security Act (ISA). Ongoing arrests are expected as authorities estimate there may be at least 100 others with extremist ties who are on the run. Most are low-level members and ground soldiers operating from *madrasahs* (Islamic schools) in the states of Johor, Pahang, and Kuala Lumpur, with little knowledge about the details of the larger plans and context of JI. Police have cautioned that even as they round up suspected KMM leaders, more *wakallahs* (KMM state leaders) are quickly taking their places. Yet, the police assure the public that while the battle against terrorism will be drawn out, the situation is well under control as "continued police vigilance [has] kept them at bay."

The Malaysian government is considering implementing a witness protection scheme to combat terrorism, possibly modeled on the U.S. example, and it will also likely establish a coast guard for further border security. The Ministry of Defense has also established a Nuclear, Biological and Chemical Defense (NBCD) unit in the army, largely in response to the past anthrax and Japanese encephalitis scares in the country but also as a unit capable of reacting to any future nuclear, biological, or chemical threats.

Despite the shock of the Bali bombings, the government has not prompted any immediate drastic tightening of security measures in Malaysia. There is concern, however, about the possibility of a similar attack in Malaysia ("local Bali") and precautionary steps have been taken to ensure a continuous high-alert status. For example, nightclub operators have been called in for security briefings with the police, patrols have been increased in busy areas, and foreign-based organizations are being watched closely.

The impending change in government leadership has led to speculation about how this might affect the country. Mahathir and Abdullah have largely laid these concerns to rest with assurances that, despite their very different styles, they share the same vision for Malaysia's future, as laid out in the nation's Vision 2020. Indeed, the country's direction appears to be set to remain on course with minimal changes to major long-term policies affecting its political and economic stability. Abdullah's leadership will increasingly become more visible, albeit subtly, as the country prepares psychologically for the imminent departure of the vocal, tough, and globally recognized prime minister who has dominated the domestic political scene for more than two decades.

Haji Hadi Awang, successor of the conservative opposition Parti Islam SeMalaysia (PAS, or the Islamic Party of Malaysia) since the sudden death of Datuk Fadzil Noor in June 2002, is being carefully watched by the political mainstream. Widely regarded as more radical than his predecessor, Hadi's stated intention of capturing more Malaysian states in the next general election prompted apprehension among many Malaysians, who see developments in PAS-governed Terengganu as a good indication of how the PAS would rule elsewhere if given a chance. The enactment of the *Hudud* bill in the state of Terengganu that prescribes a strict, and some believe, flawed, interpretation of Islamic law has come under severe scrutiny and met with strong resistance by non-Muslims and even many Muslims throughout the country. Women's groups have been particularly scathing in their review of the bill, directing their outrage toward the inadequacy and inequity of the enacted law in relation to rape. Although there continues to be considerable support for PAS by many disillusioned with the ruling coalition, specifically the United Malays National Organization (UMNO) as a party, political support for PAS has grown weaker since the September 11, 2001, terrorist attacks in the United States, which caused many Malays to shy away from parties perceived to have extremist leanings.

EXTERNAL Malaysia generally has excellent relations with neighboring countries, all of which are partners in the Association of Southeast Asian Nations (ASEAN). These relations are complicated, however, by the large number of illegal migrants from lower income countries and by episodic issues that provoke nationalistic sentiments. Strained relations with Indonesia and the Philippines developed when a three-month amnesty ended August 1, 2002, and Malaysia tightened immigration laws to include caning and deportation of illegal immigrants. The Indonesian People's Consultative Assembly speaker, Amien Rais, lashed out at the canings of those who remained illegally after the end of the waiting period as "inhumane," since Indonesia and Malaysia shared the same ethnic roots. This sparked a demonstration in Indonesia led by a group calling itself the Laskar Merah Putih (Red and White Militia), after the colors of the Indonesian flag. Protesters chanted slogans, toppled the main gate of the Malaysian embassy, and burned a Malaysian flag. Jakarta later clarified that Amien Rais's statement did not reflect the government's position, and Malaysia dismissed the flag-burning as an isolated incident. Foreign Minister Syed Hamid Albar, however, urged Malaysians to avoid traveling to Indonesia at that time due to the high emotions. Indonesia suggested that the recruitment of Indonesian labor be done on a government-to-government basis to limit problems of illegal entry. Many of the previously illegal Indonesian immigrants have since been readmitted to the country with valid passports and work permits to meet the continuing high demand for their labor, especially in the plantation and construction industries. Despite this period of tension, Indonesia-Malaysia relations remain cordial, as particularly evidenced by the outcome of the Sipadan-Ligitan dispute settled by the

International Court of Justice (ICJ), in which Malaysia won by a majority of 16 to 1. Indonesia, although disappointed, graciously accepted the decision.

In the case of the Philippines, when a 13-year-old Filipina claimed that she had been raped at a detention center in Sabah, President Gloria Macapagal Arroyo wrote to Prime Minister Mahathir requesting an investigation. The matter was blown up by the Philippine media, and then came to an embarrassing halt when it was discovered that the girl was actually a Malaysian. Kuala Lumpur demanded an apology from Manila. Even if this incident is laid to rest, relations will probably remain strained because of a Filipino intelligence official's allegation that some ruling Barisan Nasional politicians have "ideological ties" to the Moro Islamic Liberation Front (MILF) and al Qaeda. This allegation reflects underlying suspicions in Manila that Kuala Lumpur is not fully supportive of its efforts to suppress Muslim separatists in the Philippine south.

Despite the high degree of interdependence between Singapore and Malaysia and their excellent cooperation on most economic matters and terrorism, the relations between the two states are periodically troubled. For example, last year a dispute arose over the price of water that Malaysia supplies to Singapore, and media coverage and inflamed political rhetoric from both sides intensified the issue. Malaysians also resent Singapore opposition to a Malaysian proposal to establish an ASEAN + 3 (China, Japan, and South Korea) secretariat in Kuala Lumpur. The strain in bilateral ties reached a new level over the territorial dispute of Pulau Butih Puteh, a small rocky outcrop about 15 nautical miles off the southern state of Johor, claimed by both Malaysia and Singapore. Although a framework agreement has been drawn up for referral of the matter to the ICJ, settlement on a suitable date of signing continues to be a delaying factor, with both sides accusing each other of tardiness. Syed Hamid, minister of foreign affairs, voiced that for Malaysia, future ties with Singapore could be based on national interest and no longer on the principle of good neighborliness, given that both countries viewed bilateral ties from "different perspectives."

Australian Prime Minister John Howard's talk of "pre-emptive strikes" against neighbors to prevent terrorist attacks outraged Malaysians, who viewed such rhetoric as an arrogant challenge to national sovereignty. Malaysia even spoke of reviewing its Memorandum of Understanding with Australia to combat terrorism, entered into in August 2002, and Mahathir, in his New Year's address, promised that any country violating Malaysian freedom would get "what they (Westerners) call a 'bloody nose.'"

DEFENSE POLICIES AND ISSUES

DEFENSE POLICY   In line with its "defensive" posture, Malaysia remains committed to developing a well-balanced and credible defense force for countering attacks involving a wide range of circumstances beyond simply responding to low-level contingency scenarios, as in the past. The Ministry of Defense places a heavy emphasis on the core technological skills of the Malaysian Armed Forces (MAF), and it plans to revamp the MAF by adapting the military to the Revolution in Military Affairs. Although the country does not foresee the possibility of any conventional threat in the near future, the Strategic Review on Malaysia's Defense Policy calls for increased security and patrol along the coastline and a boost in conventional capabilities.

The international war on terrorism adds another dimension to Malaysia's counter-terrorist and defense efforts. With increased linkages between local extremist groups and internationally organized terrorist groups, accurate intelligence and the timely exchange of information with other nations is seen as a key element in effective counter-terrorism. Indeed, Malaysia's defense policy is now being redefined after September 11, although details remain confidential. Malaysia has also been reviewing its priorities for its international security and defense relationship. While Malaysia's alliances with the major Western powers continue to be traditionally strong, as does its ties to Southeast Asian neighbors, the fact that Northeast Asia remains a potential regional flashpoint has led to increasing military links between Malaysia and China. Navy vessels from both countries have paid goodwill visits, and they are considering the possibility of joint military exercises. Closer cooperation, still in its exploratory stages, seems logical given China's rising prominence in the region and the world.

FORCE STRUCTURE AND TRADING   The Malaysian army is continuing to downsize through attrition from its current strength of 80,000 to 70,000 personnel. There are currently about 40,000 reservists, although the majority of these are former army personnel who may be recalled during an emergency. The reduction in regular forces is to be offset by a planned reservist force of about 100,000 personnel. In light of the new equipment being introduced to the MAF, the Defense Ministry is promoting MAF as a learning organization so as to attract skilled, quality personnel. Training is geared toward ensuring personnel can use sophisticated weaponry and on developing "Knowledge-Soldiers (K-soldiers)." The ministry is also creating more training opportunities abroad, through existing bilateral defense linkages and major procurements, especially in areas where the MAF lacks expertise.

MAF priorities center on integrating three military elements—intelligence, command systems, and surveillance—into a unified system giving commanders a complete picture of the battlefield and enhancing MAF responses in near real-time, around the clock. MAF is also making significant progress in its combined arms doctrine, which will allow it to raise its first Combined Arms Division in the future. The Malaysian army also plans to make extensive use of computer-based training tools for combined arms training in the southern state of Johor. Integral to the Division will be assets such as main battle tanks, armored infantry fighting vehicles, multiple-barrel rocket launchers, shoulder-launched and short-range air defense missile systems, anti-armor guided missiles, and light observation helicopters.

The Royal Malaysian Navy (RMN) continues to expand its naval aviation and undersea warfare capabilities; a new naval aviation base is being built nine miles from the RMN's major naval base at Lumut. The Royal Malaysian Air Force (RMAF) is focusing on developing its electronic warfare (EW) capability. It established an EW center in 1993, and hopes to convince the army and the navy to coordinate EW capabilities. Although the RMAF will continue to operate medium-lift helicopters for combat search-and-rescue purposes, it is now eager to undertake heavy-lift helicopter roles and refine its offensive air superiority potential by procuring up to 16 multi-role combat aircraft.

DEFENSE BUDGET AND PROCUREMENT   Despite the RM400 million (US$104 million at RM1 = US$0.26) increase in allocation to the Defense Ministry under the 2003 budget, the defense budget, at approximately 2.5 percent of gross domestic product, is still small compared to that of most Asia Pacific countries. With the increased allocation, major equipment procurement, suspended following the 1997 Asian financial crisis, will now go forward.

At the eighth Defense Services Asia 2002 Exhibition and Conference in April, Malaysia signed seven letters of agreement for equipment procurement. Among them were a regiment-strong Jernas enhanced short-range air defense system worth RM1.18 billion (US$306.8 million), a BR-90 Combat Support Bridging System worth RM113.245 million (US$29.44 million), a tactical floating bridge worth RM106.92 (US$27.8 million), 24,000 Steyr assault rifles worth RM84.48 million (US$21.96 million), and a proposed RM76 million (US$19.76 million) production of 25 mm Bushmaster Bullets for the new Malaysian armored combat vehicle, the ACV 300 Kepada Adnan. The Malaysian army officially took delivery of the first of 211 FNSS ACV 300 Kepada Adnans ordered two years ago.

The army is the recipient of most of the new weaponry. It is presently undergoing transformation from a largely anti-guerilla and anti-terrorist jungle force into a fully conventional force, while retaining jungle warfare capabilities. Currently equipped with the Thales Starburst and Anza Mk2 Man-Portable Air Defense Systems (MANPADS), the army is expected to equip at least four of its infantry battalions with the Russian IGLA-1 9K310 MANPADS to enhance the role of the Jernas missile systems, at a contract value of RM182 million (US$47.32 million). This will make the Malaysian army the sixth member of ASEAN to acquire the IGLA family of MANPADS besides Cambodia, Laos, Myanmar, Singapore, and Vietnam. An agreement for 48 Polish PT-91 Main Battle Tanks and 14 support vehicles, including simulators, for the establishment of a main battle tank regiment is also expected to be signed by the end of 2002. The deal, which will involve counter-trade as part payment, would include armored recovery engineering and bridge launching vehicles based on the same chassis as the PT-91. The first batch of tanks will be delivered in 2004. The planned purchase of attack helicopters for the Army Air Wing will now be deferred due to lack of funds and experienced pilots. Instead, the Wing is scheduled to be equipped with 10 Light Overvation helicopters. The helicopters, to be used for utility, reconnaissance, and fire support, will replace the Wing's current mount purchased in the 1960s, the Alouette III.

The RMN will upgrade the Command and Control System (CCS) on two Laksamana-class corvettes—the KD *Laksamana Hang Nadim* and KD *Laksamana Tun Abdul Jamil*—at a contract value of US$15 million. It has also ordered control systems for six new MEKO 100 patrol vessels, at a cost of US$37.08 million, with delivery expected to take place by the end of 2004. The RMN has also commissioned European shipbuilders DCNI of France and Izar of Spain to build two new Scorpene-class submarines armed with Exocet SM 39 missiles and a Thales weapons system, giving Malaysia a submarine fleet. The agreement, signed in June, will supply an overhauled ex-French Navy Agosta 70–class submarine for a six-year period of training. The purchase cost will be RM3.1 billion (US$806 million) to RM3.4 billion (US$884 million) with staggered payments over a six- or seven-year time frame. France will buy US$223.82 million worth of Malaysian palm oil and US$89.53 million of other Malaysian-made commodities, and invest US$134.29 million for training and technology transfer to Malaysian firms.

Contributions to Regional and Global Security

Despite the political differences between Malaysia and its neighbors over certain issues, security and intelligence cooperation in the campaign against terrorism remains strong with all ASEAN countries. Indonesia, the Philippines, and Malaysia have signed a trilateral pact, Exchange of Information and Establishment of Communication Procedures, which is expected to improve information exchange on cross-border terrorist activities. Malaysia also works closely with its Thai counterparts in keeping close tabs on suspected Malaysian JI members working with their colleagues in similar organizations in southern Thailand. To avoid bureaucratic delays, the Malaysian police have established a joint hotline with Philippine counterparts to combat cross-border terrorism and the entry of illegal immigrants in each country. The RMN, alert to the possibility that ships could be targeted in terror attacks, also co-operates closely in sharing intelligence with the U.S. and Indian navies patrolling the Strait of Malacca, one of the world's busiest shipping lanes. In addition, Malaysia is also fully supportive of participation in the U.S. Customs Service's Container Security Initiative, under which cargo destined for the United States is pre-screened at Malaysian ports.

After discussions in July with visiting U.S. Secretary of State Colin Powell, Malaysian government leaders are considering with the United States plans to set up a joint anti-terrorism training center to instruct Southeast Asian security services on how to combat terrorism.

Through ASEAN, Malaysia is a party to the ASEAN-U.S. Joint Declaration for Cooperation to Combat International Terrorism as well as the Joint Communiqué of the Special ASEAN Meeting on Terrorism, which called for the execution of the Work Program on Terrorism to Implement the ASEAN Plan of Action to Combat Transnational Crime.

Generally, the United States and Malaysia have had excellent cooperation in the campaign against terrorism. For example, Malaysia deported the suspected American terrorist Ahmad Ibrahim Bilal and agreed to allow the FBI to question Malaysian Yazid Sufaat on his link to the September 11 hijackers. Malaysia, however, does not support all elements of the American approach to counter-terrorism and containment of weapons of mass destruction. The Malaysian government is unwilling, for example, to lend any support to a war in Iraq because it believes that such an attack will only further inflame Muslim sentiments, already heightened since September 11. Malaysia does, however, support full UN inspections in Iraq.

Malaysia will head the Non-Aligned Movement and will host the Organization of Islamic Conference Summit in 2003. At this forum and others, it will raise its concerns about deficiencies in addressing the root causes of terrorism.

_11_ Mongolia

THE SECURITY ENVIRONMENT

More than a decade has passed since Mongolia embarked upon the road toward democracy and began the transition to an open-market economy. Although the transition has not always been smooth, Mongolia has succeeded in making significant economic, political, and social reforms in a relatively short period. By strengthening relations with neighboring China and Russia and extending cooperation to all countries of the Asia Pacific region, Mongolia has also enjoyed a beneficial external security environment. Therefore, government policy priorities increasingly emphasize nontraditional security issues such as economic development, ecological balance, and other human security challenges.

INTERNAL The Mongolian People's Revolutionary Party (MPRP) returned to power in the 2000 elections, winning an absolute majority in the Great State Hural (parliament) and thus becoming the governing party without a need for coalition partners. To maintain its political position in Mongolia's democratic environment, the major challenge for the MPRP is to implement its ambitious election promises: tripling the minimum wage and doubling civil service salaries, pensions, and allowances, while also reducing the tax burden on businesses by 30 percent, alleviating poverty, and decreasing unemployment and the large budget deficit. Although the government has made important strides toward ensuring stable economic development and improving welfare through an acceleration of economic reforms as well as reducing the budget deficits, there are still many underlying problems. The economy has a relatively narrow base: livestock and agriculture; mining (gold, copper, and flour-spar); export of skins, hides, wool, and cashmere; and international assistance. Harsh climatic conditions, droughts, and fires have caused heavy losses in the livestock and agricultural industries in recent years, and the drop in world prices for Mongolia's copper and wool exports have reduced foreign exchange earnings. The net result has been growth, but not at the desired level.

To strengthen economic performance, the government designated 2002 as a Year of Investment Promotion and undertook a series of initiatives such as the 3rd Mongolia: Investors' Forum-2002 in Ulaanbaatar in September 2002 with more than 1,100 participants. These efforts will continue. In addition, as another source of foreign exchange, Mongolia is emphasizing tourism, especially ecotourism, and has declared 2003 Visit Mongolia Year.

EXTERNAL   For obvious reasons, the development of relations with the Russian Federation and the People's Republic of China remain at the top of Mongolia's foreign policy priorities. Relations with both giant neighbors have progressed smoothly. Russian President Vladimir Putin's visit in 2000 ushered in a new phase in Russo-Mongolian relations. The two presidents signed the Ulaanbaatar Declaration, an important document that reflects mutual interests in developing relations to meet the challenges and goals of the new century, based on strict observance of the 1993 Treaty on Friendship and Cooperation.

Russian Prime Minister Mikhail Kasyanov's visit to Ulaanbaatar in March 2002 continued the momentum and showed that the two countries take identical positions on many contemporary international issues. Mongolia and Russia pledged to support each other's efforts, initiatives, and concrete measures to safeguard peace and strengthen security in the region. During the visit, a number of important documents, such as a Consular Convention, a note on approval of documents on the results of Mongolian-Russian border inspection, agreements on cooperation on natural gas issues, and protocol on trade and economic cooperation, were signed.

Despite the highly positive tone of political relations with Russia, economic relations continue to need development. Russia is a major trading partner, but the list of traded products is short, confined mainly to Mongolian mineral exports and Russian petroleum products and machine spare parts. Mongolians believe that high Russian customs duties are a significant deterrent to Mongolian exports. The issue of

Mongolia's debt to Russia also remains unresolved despite strong expectations at the time of the Kasyanov visit. The Russians have expressed their desire to solve the issue without adversely affecting Mongolia's economy, but the previous forms of handling debt in the socialist era are no longer applicable.

Relations with China have been significantly deepened with regular high-level exchanges. Chinese leaders have emphasized time and again that they respect whatever path of development is chosen by Mongolia, and they have remained faithful to the position of promoting friendly relations regardless of political changes in Mongolia.

There are no unresolved matters of principle between Mongolia and China, and the two sides believe that any problem that may arise between them can be resolved through dialogue in a friendly manner. The absence of political, legal, and historical problems and conflicts of interests between the two countries create excellent conditions for enhancing their relationship.

Sino-Mongolian economic cooperation is growing rapidly. China is Mongolia's largest trading partner and investor. Mongolia imports food products, consumer goods, and construction materials from China, while about 80 percent of its exports are unrefined natural raw materials and unprocessed materials of animal origin.

Mongolian Prime Minister Nambaryn Enkhbayar visited Beijing in January 2002 to reassure China of its high place in Mongolian foreign policy and to secure economic assistance for some of the MPRP-initiated projects. The prime minister proposed a railway link between the eastern province of Mongolia and the northeastern region of China, furthering the cooperation in mining and increasing Chinese investment in Mongolia's infrastructure.

Mongolian-Chinese joint ventures mainly focus on construction projects, retail sales, and food services. Lately, Chinese investment is increasingly directed into animal husbandry and agriculture. Although China is the largest foreign investor by total amount invested, the value of Chinese investment is reduced by several factors. Most small Chinese investors are seeking long-term residence permits rather than investing and conducting business. Moreover, the low initial capital requirement for registration makes it easy for Chinese to register a joint venture but actually engage in other activities. Most Chinese businesses established in Mongolia are small-scale, technologically poor, and directed toward buying raw materials as cheaply as possible in order to export them to China for higher value-added processing.

Notwithstanding routine high-level visits and pledges of economic cooperation, there are sensitivities in Sino-Mongolian relations, mostly reflecting internal issues in China. Despite Mongolia's commitment to the "one China" principle, Beijing keeps a wary eye on the Ulaanbaatar-Taipei relationship. The opening of a Taiwanese trade representative office in Ulaanbaatar, the expansion of economic ties with Taiwan, and Taipei's recognition of Mongolia's sovereignty in 2002 created suspicions in Beijing. A second issue is related to Chinese opposition to visits of the Dalai Lama to Mongolia. In August 2002, because of Chinese pressure, Russia and South Korea refused to provide transit visas to the Dalai Lama to visit Mongolia for purely religious purposes. In November, when the Dalai Lama visited Mongolia via Tokyo, both Beijing and Moscow reacted negatively. During the Dalai Lama's visit, China closed the railway border-crossing with Mongolia for several days for "technical" reasons. Just after the visit, Russia raised a debt issue.

There is no doubt that friendly relations and mutually beneficial cooperation with China offer Mongolia greater possibilities to integrate itself into the world economy, but from a less optimistic point of view, these may lead Mongolia to be heavily dependent on China. Accordingly, while giving priority to its immediate neighbors, Mongolia seeks good relations and cooperation with other influential powers like the United States, Japan, the United Kingdom, Germany, and South Korea, not just for their own value but also as credible counterweights to Russia and China. The concept of the "third neighbor" includes not only Western but also East Asian nations and even India. South Korea and Japan are third neighbors in economic terms, the United States is a third neighbor in strategic terms, and India is a third neighbor in a cultural sense. In recent years, Japan's economic cooperation has shifted from emergency- and humanitarian-based assistance to a more basic and longer-term capacity and to infrastructural building programs. Mongolians regard broadening relations with the United States as important for consolidation of Mongolia's democracy and the success of the country's market-economy reforms.

DEFENSE POLICIES AND ISSUES

Due to its favorable external environment, Mongolia is able to conduct an independent and neutral defense policy in harmony with its national interests and self-defense principles and norms. The content, principles, objectives, and directions of the defense policy are based on key documents including the Constitution of Mongolia, defense and defense-related laws and acts, the National Security and Foreign Policy Concepts, and the Fundamentals of State Military Policy.

Mongolia has a small, capable, and professionally oriented armed forces in line with its defense needs and economic size. The defense budget is about 6 percent of the national budget and 2 percent of the gross domestic product. The budget is likely to remain the same in the future. The defense budget will grow with the increase of national economic capabilities, but there are no current pressures in Mongolia's external or internal environments to expand the share of the national budget devoted to defense.

With the favorable external environment and democratic changes taking place in the country, the missions of the armed forces are becoming more humanitarian. In addition to countering any potential aggression, the Mongolian armed forces emphasize border security and disaster relief. Training programs reflect these new priorities. In addition, as will be described later, Mongolia believes it can play an enhanced role in UN peacekeeping operations.

Another emphasis of defense policy is to foster military diplomacy to create trust with other countries' armed forces and broaden security cooperation. Besides the deepening of military-to-military relations with its neighbors, Mongolia actively seeks to expand military ties with other nations including the United States, Germany, Belgium, Turkey, and Switzerland.

CONTRIBUTIONS TO REGIONAL AND GLOBAL SECURITY

In line with its open foreign policy, Mongolia is seeking to enhance its participation in international affairs. It is active in regional and international organizations and in track two processes. As a small nation, Mongolia has a strong national interest in the development of a stable global order, and for this reason supports international efforts to eliminate terrorism and international preventive diplomacy, peacekeeping, and nation building.

Mongolia has a special interest in promoting mutual understanding and cooperation and peace and stability in Northeast Asia. Pursuing a multi-pronged, open, and proactive foreign policy, the government of Mongolia has sought, in accordance with the Concept of Mongolia's

Foreign Policy as well as its Program of Action, to develop closer relations of friendship and cooperation with the countries of the subregion. The government sees such enhanced relations within Northeast Asia as a bridge through which Mongolia can eventually contribute to mutual understanding, a stable peace, and development in the larger Asia Pacific region and the world.

The economic and social stability of Northeast Asia is the foundation for Mongolia's political and military stability. For this reason, Mongolia attaches great importance to regional economic cooperation. Its participation in the Tumen River project and the Pacific Economic Cooperation Council (PECC) and its aspirations to join the Asia-Pacific Economic Cooperation (APEC) forum are motivated not only by its interest in mutually beneficial economic cooperation but also by the political importance of such cooperation.

The Mongolian government believes that the lack of a multilateral security dialogue mechanism in Northeast Asia has inhibited the ability of countries in the subregion to address some of the security issues left over from the cold war era. Mongolia would like to see the discussion of Northeast Asian security issues institutionalized and has suggested this in the ASEAN Regional Forum (ARF). Its own experience of friendly relations with both North and South Korea encourages the Mongolian belief that a regional mechanism can help address problems in this difficult bilateral relationship. Mongolia supports the further involvement of North Korea in a regional security multilateral dialogue.

Track two activities are an essential part of the efforts to strengthen peace and confidence building. Ulaanbaatar co-hosted a Symposium on Northeast Asian Security in June and the 8th Plenary Meeting of the Expanded Senior Panel on Limited Nuclear Weapon-Free Zone for Northeast Asia in July 2002. At the broader Asia Pacific level, Mongolia hosted in July the 7th Asia Pacific Regional Peace Operations Seminar-Game, in cooperation with the United Nations and the U.S. Center for Excellence in Disaster Management and Humanitarian Assistance. The seminar-game promoted regional cooperation on issues of security and conflict prevention, while helping build regional peace operations.

October 2002 saw the celebration of the 40th Anniversary of Mongolia's UN membership. The anniversary helped highlight the contribution of Mongolia toward the search for solutions to common issues of peace and security, such as its initiatives on the annual Disarmament Week and the 1984 UN Declaration of the Right of Peoples to Peace, which are conducted to promote disarmament goals. UN Secretary General Kofi Annan visited Ulaanbaatar at the time of this anniversary, and the potential for greater involvement of Mongolian military personnel in UN peacekeeping operations was one important item of discussion. Mongolia already is intensively preparing its military for UN peacekeeping operations. A platoon from Mongolia recently took part in international peacekeeping field training held in Bangladesh. The first observers from Mongolia are involved in peacekeeping operations in the Congo. The secretary general expressed his support for greater involvement in peacekeeping as well as for the establishment of a peacekeeping training center in Ulaanbaatar.

The full implementation of the UN General Assembly resolution on "Mongolia's international security and nuclear-weapon-free status," adopted in 2000, will be a significant contribution to regional and global security. Mongolia is actively pursuing the implementation of the resolution. Currently, it is holding consultations with the relevant nuclear powers on the basic elements of a treaty that would, if concluded, institutionalize its nuclear-weapon-free status.

The terrorist attacks of September 11, 2001, in the United States demonstrated the need for and importance of closer international cooperation against terrorism. Mongolia joined the global coalition against international terrorism without any reservations and expressed its readiness to contribute to the global fight against terrorism in any possible way. It is taking all possible measures to implement the resolutions of the UN General Assembly and the Security Council as well as relevant international agreements on terrorism. It was the first country to report to the Security Council on its measures.

Finally, an enabling international environment and successful domestic development are inseparably connected. The government of Mongolia regards its own policy of economic and political reforms in accordance with its Program of Action as not just contributing to its own national well-being, but as a domestic building block of regional and global order. To indicate what it is doing and to facilitate exchanges of experience, Mongolia is hosting the Fifth International Conference of New or Restored Democracies in 2003.

In his report to the 57th session of the UN General Assembly on Mongolia's International Security and Nuclear Weapon Free Status,

Kofi Annan remarked that the steadily improving prospects for democratic governance, transparency, and participation and the rule of law in Mongolia contribute to a more stable security situation in the whole region. This may be Mongolia's most important contribution to the security of the subregion in addition to its other relevant efforts and initiatives such as nuclear-weapon-free status.

12 New Zealand

The Security Environment

The lingering aftereffects of the September 11, 2001, terrorist attacks in the United States, the emergence of Islamist terrorism activity in Southeast Asia, and the October 12, 2002, Bali bombings in particular are altering popular perceptions of New Zealand's security environment. Gone is the notion that New Zealand is an isolated and safe place free from the threat of terrorist attack. The Bali bombings have stimulated a questioning of the government's defense policy by editorial writers, opposition parties, and radio talk shows. A cabinet member's admission that New Zealand's antinuclear policy may prevent it from reaching a free-trade agreement with the United States also helped spark the first real skepticism of the country's "independent" foreign policy since the mid-1980s.

The new view, however, is not reflected in New Zealand's limited academia and media circles, which generally cling to traditional left wing interpretations of what drives international affairs and how New Zealand should respond. New Zealand has no think tanks dealing with external affairs, and with the exception of one university, diplomatic history is no longer taught at New Zealand universities. Realist-grounded international and strategic affairs are no longer fashionable in the university. As for the media, New Zealand lacks specialist foreign affairs and defense journalists. Despite this, New Zealand journalists are independently minded and have raised searching questions about New Zealand's "independent" foreign policy. This questioning is unlikely to be sustained in part as external affairs issues generally fail to hold the attention of the media but perhaps more importantly because local journalists tend to be nationalistic in a defensive way.

Nor is the questioning likely to significantly sway official perceptions of security and defense issues as the Labour-led coalition government retained office (with a slightly increased majority) in the July 2002 elections. This government is dominated by ministers who hold strong views on the international world and New Zealand's appropriate foreign and defense policies, and there is little likelihood that these will change. Nor is there any serious chance that New Zealand will alter its antinuclear stance in the immediate future. The opposition led by the conservative National Party supports the Labour Party view that the antinuclear policy is an integral pillar of New Zealand's emerging fragile national identity.

INTERNAL   The government's assessment of domestic security is that New Zealand is unlikely to be faced with the threat of direct attack from any state and that the security environment is benign, but that terrorism and espionage have to be taken seriously. A measure of New Zealand's approach to internal security is provided in the annual report of the Security Intelligence Service (SIS) to Parliament. The SIS states that the threat of terrorism is low, but events such as a visit by a high-profile overseas visitor or a large international gathering could be regarded by overseas terrorists as "providing the opportunity to do something spectacular to capture world-wide publicity." The SIS also believes that the threat of espionage and foreign interference is present in New Zealand: "Intelligence officers are still sent from foreign countries to pursue objectives detrimental" to the interests of New Zealand and "intelligence organisations target New Zealand interests elsewhere in the world." Moreover, "individuals and groups in New Zealand have links to terrorist organisations overseas." Some of these have "developed local structures that are dedicated to the support of their overseas parent bodies."

Prime Minister Helen Clark has emphasized that the events in Bali highlight the continuing threat of international terrorism and the need to work closely within the Asia Pacific region and globally to counter this threat. According to the prime minister, the "most important contribution New Zealand can make to this global effort against terrorism is through intelligence and security measures. The government is determined to do everything it can to thwart terrorism. Terrorism has no boundaries. It can strike any place at any time."

Since September 11, the government has committed an extra NZ$30 million (US$15.6 million at NZ$1 = US$0.52) over three years to agencies involved in counter-terrorism and border protection. Aviation security measures have been strengthened for international flights and for domestic travel on larger commercial aircraft. Border protection has been enhanced by customs, immigration, and the police. The agencies responsible for foreign and domestic intelligence have received small budget increases, and the SIS has been expanded from 100 to 140 officers. Police liaison officers have been appointed in London and Washington, and a small intelligence unit within the police department has been formed to counter terrorism. A capability to respond to chemical or biological terrorist emergencies has been established in the defense force although so far there appears to be no capacity to deal with radiological or nuclear terrorism. A Terrorism Suppression Act was passed in Parliament with bipartisan support, and further legislation is being prepared that will criminalize unlawful possession of plastic explosives and nuclear materials, and certain terrorist acts including attacks on the food chain or bio-terrorism. This act will also serve to strengthen international information-sharing between border agencies.

Questions have been raised by the media and opposition parties about the extent and quality of New Zealand's intelligence links with the United States and Australia in the wake of the Bali bombings. Acting Prime Minister Michael Cullen said that New Zealand did not receive any warning about the possibility of impending attacks on foreigners in Bali as intelligence assessments were too vague and lacked detail; consequently, there were no warnings to receive.

EXTERNAL   Of New Zealand's external security relationships, that with Australia remains its closest and most important. Despite the dramatic changes in New Zealand's defense posture since late 1999 (outlined in *Asian Pacific Security Outlook 2001* and *2002*) and the country's virtual withdrawal from the defense of Australia, the trans-Tasman defense linkage has been maintained.

New Zealand and Australia have agreed to work more closely on peacekeeping training, activities in the South Pacific, and coastal-maritime patrol and surveillance activities. Special forces cooperation remains close and Special Air Service (SAS) soldiers from both countries worked along side each other in operations such as ANACONDA in Afghanistan. New Zealand and Australia also have maintained cooperation on combined logistics and support. The two countries worked closely in peacekeeping in East Timor, where New Zealand maintained an infantry battalion from October 1999 to December 2002. This battalion and its supported air force helicopter contingent operated continuously along with Australian forces on the border of East Timor.

The Bali bombing incident also contributed to a sense of trans-Tasman affinity. New Zealanders were shocked by the scale of the bombing, and there was widespread spontaneous though understated sympathy and compassion expressed for all who were killed and wounded. The Bali bombings killed at least three New Zealanders with many others wounded. New Zealand's response included the dispatch of C-130 Hercules aircraft in an aeromedical evacuation role, which was integrated with Australian and Indonesian efforts.

Some evidence of friction in the relationship emerged in 2002. Foreign Minister Philip Goff asked his counterpart Alexander Downer to stop Australian diplomatic efforts to undermine New Zealand's negotiation of a free-trade agreement in Washington. However, Downer's visit to New Zealand in December 2002 hosted by Goff appeared to be characterized by good atmospherics.

Differential treatment by the United States of Australia and New Zealand regarding free trade reminded New Zealanders that while relations with the United States have normalized, they will not be treated in Washington as if they remain an alliance partner. When Prime Minister Clark visited Washington in March 2002 and met with President George W. Bush, Secretary of State Colin Powell, and other senior officials, the New Zealand government interpreted the reception as evidence of a further warming in the bilateral relationship and a signal of the U.S. appreciation for New Zealand's contributions to the war on terrorism. When asked, Powell described the relationship as one of "very, very" good friends. On the face of it, the visit appeared to be a diplomatic and political triumph for Clark. She had been the driving force behind New Zealand's antinuclear legislation and the reorientation of New Zealand's foreign policy from that of a trusted ally of the United States to that of an "independent" state with a security focus on the South Pacific and peacekeeping.

In October, however, Deputy Prime Minister and Minister of Finance Michael Cullen returned from the United States and reported that New Zealand's antinuclear stance placed New Zealand well down the queue of states lining up for free-trade deals with the United States. Cullen said that it was explained to him that Australia's strategic relationship made the difference in the U.S. response to that country. Some believe that the U.S. reluctance can also be explained by New Zealand's strategic stance on the war on terrorism. While New Zealand provided Special Forces for Afghanistan, its position on Iraq differs significantly from that of the United States and Australia.

Cullen's admission led to questioning by the media of the relevance and cost of the antinuclear policy. Foreign Minister Goff put the cost of New Zealand's exclusion from a free-trade deal at NZ$1 billion (US$520 million) a year. Economics and business commentators suggested that there would be additional costs as Australia would gain a competitive edge over New Zealand business. Both Cullen and Goff stressed that an Australian-U.S. free-trade agreement was far from a done deal and that U.S. officials had said that New Zealand would still be on the list of those states being considered for a free-trade deal even though progress would be unlikely in the short term.

The extent to which the bilateral relationship with the United States may be strained by differences over Iraq is far from clear. New Zealand adopts the stance that Iraq must comply with the UN Security Council's demands for inspection for weapons of mass destruction, and that Security Council resolutions cannot be constantly flouted with impunity. Should Iraq fail to fully comply with the inspection regime, the Council will need to make a clear decision on further action. While New Zealand does not rule out the use of force, it maintains that this must be authorized by the Security Council as a whole.

Goff said that New Zealand will consider offering humanitarian help, such as medical units, to a war with Iraq, if the war had multilateral support sanctioned by the United Nations.

One reason cited by the government to explain New Zealand's coolness about contributing combat forces to Iraq is that military personnel are exhausted from their contributions to East Timor and Afghanistan. Other relevant naval and air force combat force elements (a frigate and two P3K Orion aircraft) that could be made available for the war on Iraq have already been contributed to a Canadian-led anti-terrorism maritime task force operating in the Persian Gulf.

Until late 1999, the Five Power Defense Arrangements (FPDA) exercises and activities based in Malaysia and Singapore were one of the main drivers of New Zealand's external defense policy and relations. Southeast Asia was viewed as strategically important to New Zealand, and New Zealand's interests were seen as being integrated with those of Southeast Asia and East Asia more broadly. The Clark administration prefers not to frame policy responses in terms of national interest and has generally tried to distance itself from a defense profile in Southeast Asia. The government is not comfortable with Asian security issues. This approach appears to be based, at least in part, on the view that certain Asian states are still governed by repressive regimes. The extent to which this stance will be modified, if at all, in light of the Bali bombings and evidence of active Islamist terrorist activity in Southeast Asia remains to be seen.

DEFENSE POLICIES AND ISSUES

New Zealand's defense reorientation is unlikely to swing back to more traditional approaches to defense planning for the foreseeable future. The nature and form of national security change was outlined in *Asia Pacific Security Outlook 2001* and *2002*.

Goff said in early 2003 that advice received from the defense force indicated that both the conventional and special forces needed time to regenerate and regroup following demanding tours of duty in East Timor and Afghanistan. The situation is also a consequence of the quantitative and qualitative decline in the capacity of New Zealand's defense force since the mid-1980s caused by budget cuts (defense spending has fallen from 1.8 percent of gross domestic product to around 1.0 percent) and cuts in capability (two frigates, medium artillery, armored reconnaissance, tactical transport, the air combat force, and the anti-submarine warfare capability of the P3K Orions). When the limited pool of remaining force elements gets exhausted from strenuous deployment, there are few other options available to the government to cover other contingencies.

The capabilities that remain are mostly funded in the ten-year long-term defense capital plan approved by the government early in 2002. The plan earmarks NZ$2 billion (US$1.04 billion) for major defense projects over the next decade (by way of comparison, New Zealand will spend about 5 percent of what Australia spends). The plan focuses on capabilities relevant to coastal watch duties, peacekeeping, and logistic support.

Funding was approved for the government in 2002 for a variety of major capital projects that will be completed over the next ten years and will include upgrade of five C-130 aircraft (NZ$100 million–NZ$170 million [US$52 million–US$88.4 million]), replacement of two Boeing 727 aircraft with two Boeing 757-200s (NZ$100 million–NZ$200 million [US$52 million–US$104 million]), upgrade of P3K Orion mission systems (NZ$150 million–NZ$220 million [US$78 million–US$114.4 million]), upgrade of C-130 and P3K communications and navigation systems (NZ$320 million [US$166.4 million]), replacement of 14 Iroquois utility helicopters (NZ$410 million [US$213.2 million]), the purchase of new multirole vessels and patrol ships (NZ$500 million [US$250 million]), and 24 automatic grenade launchers and 24 Javelin anti-armor systems for the army (NZ$37 million [US$19.24 million]).

CONTRIBUTIONS TO REGIONAL AND GLOBAL SECURITY

The infantry battalion and helicopter squadron committed to security duties on the sensitive border between East Timor and Indonesia were withdrawn in November 2002. Training assistance will continue to be provided to the East Timor Defense Force by New Zealand. New Zealand will provide observers to the United Nations effort in East Timor.

Fifteen to 19 staffers remain committed to the Bougainville peace monitoring team. New Zealand's involvement in the Solomon Islands peace-monitoring effort has finished.

New Zealand continued to participate in FPDA exercises with Australia. New Zealand's contributions to regional security with Australia, Singapore, and Malaysia have reduced both quantitatively and qualitatively following the disbandment of the air combat force and the reduction of the navy to a two-frigate force.

New Zealand committed an unspecified number of SAS soldiers (estimated to be about 30 soldiers) to Afghanistan in support of the United States–led war on terrorism. New Zealand was unable to sustain this deployment and the SAS were withdrawn in December 2002. The tours of the small teams of air movements specialists and engineers to Afghanistan expired in late 2002. Four staff officers are posted to the International Security Force in Kabul and a small number of staff officers (two to three) are posted to the U.S. Central Command.

Elsewhere, New Zealand has contributed ten communications and medical specialists to a UN weapons inspection team in Iraq and provides a small number of mine disposal specialists to the UN mine disposal efforts in Cambodia, Laos, and Mozambique. An observer is posted to the UN effort in Kosovo and another observer in Prevlaka. Two observers are posted to Sierra Leone, and 26 transport specialists remain committed to the multinational force in the Sinai. Seven observers are posted to the United Nations Truce Supervisory Organization (UNTSO) in Jerusalem.

_13_ Papua New Guinea

THE SECURITY ENVIRONMENT

INTERNAL   After coming through a difficult election year, Papua New Guinea continues to face substantial short- and long-term challenges, with a large budgetary deficit, negative economic growth, continuing problems of rural and urban lawlessness, and a need to counter corruption and restore good governance. The country's seventh post-independence elections in June 2002 somewhat unexpectedly brought Sir Michael Somare, the first prime minister following independence, back into power. Somare is leader of the National Alliance Party and architect of a broad-based coalition.

The electoral process itself was chaotic. The elections were the first to be conducted under the provisions of the recently enacted Organic Law on the Integrity of Political Parties and Candidates. Despite ambitious hopes that the new law might strengthen Papua New Guinea's chronically weak party system and reduce the large and growing number of standing candidates, 2,875 candidates—a new record—contested the 109 parliamentary seats. Of the 43 parties that registered under the new legislation, most lacked a significant support base. In the end, no party gained more than 19 seats in the parliament.

The election process itself was deeply flawed—marred by administrative breakdowns, cheating, and widespread violence, to the extent that some commentators, both within Papua New Guinea and outside, began to question the continued viability of democracy in this small, diverse country. The electoral rolls were "in a mess," according to the outgoing prime minister, polling was frequently delayed by lack of transport or ballot papers, and electoral officials and police were often unable to prevent widespread intimidation and fraud. By early August, when results were finally declared, more than 30 election-related deaths had been recorded. Eighty-three petitions have since been lodged with the court of disputed returns challenging the outcome of elections in 66 of the 103 declared seats.

Despite the chaos, when the National Parliament met in August, Somare was unanimously elected with 88 votes. With this majority, and the new restrictions on Members of Parliament (MPs) switching political allegiance, he may become the first prime minister to survive a full parliamentary term in office. He also enjoys considerable international support. Even though Australian political leaders had made clear their hopes that outgoing prime minister Sir Mekere Morauta would be re-elected, Australia was quick to welcome Somare's victory and assure him of Australia's continuing support (including bilateral aid of around US$160 million a year), at the same time urging him to maintain the momentum of ongoing political and economic reforms. In August, Australia's Prime Minister John Howard paid an official visit to Papua New Guinea. The World Bank also promised continued assistance.

The maintenance of national order and unity remains the most basic security concern. One perennial area of concern is the populous highlands provinces of the interior, while Bougainville remains another.

Even before independence in 1975, there was a resurgence of intergroup (or "tribal") fighting in the highlands, where in some areas government administration was not established until well into the 1960s. The first of a series of states of emergency in this area was declared in 1979. In recent years, intergroup fighting has further escalated with automatic weapons replacing bows and arrows, and local politicians often playing an active role. Police mobile squads, frequently outnumbered and outgunned, have proved unable to quell the fighting, and in some instances have probably aggravated the situation. In 2001, it was reported that some 1,000 people had died in intergroup fighting in Enga province over the previous four years, and fighting continued there in 2002. In the Southern Highlands, intense inter-clan fighting has been going on for more than three years. Notwithstanding the signing of a ceasefire in March 2002, the estimated death toll from recent conflicts is in the hundreds.

Apart from the loss of lives and displacement of people, and the destruction of houses and gardens, the Southern Highlands conflicts have resulted in the closure and in some cases destruction of schools, hospitals, and government offices, the blocking of roads and airstrips, the shutting down of supermarkets and stores, the temporary closure of the Porgera gold and copper mine (which over the past decade has contributed about 16 percent of Papua New Guinea's total export earnings), and threats to the lucrative Hides and Gobe gas fields. More generally, such turbulence impacts negatively on the foreign investment needed to sustain the country's failing economy.

On the eve of the 2002 national election, Southern Highlands leaders called for the Papua New Guinea Defense Force (PNGDF) to maintain order in the province, which former PNGDF commander Ted Diro had described as "totally out of control." Forces were sent after polling had commenced, but they could not end the fighting. Failed elections were declared in six of the province's nine electorates, and the PNGDF deployments continue into 2003.

In contrast, a fragile peace remains in Bougainville, long the scene of an active secessionist-minded insurgency. The 2001 Bougainville Agreement, the culmination of years of negotiations, gives the province a high level of autonomy. In 2002, passage of legislation to implement the agreement was the major achievement. With reconciliation processes continuing at the local level and the weapons disposal program said to be progressing well, the Bougainville Constitutional Development Commission began a process of popular consultation as part of the provincial constitution-making process toward the end of the year. The United Nations representative in Bougainville has warned, however, that a "very precarious" law and order situation on Bougainville poses a persistent threat to the peace process.

EXTERNAL   Externally, Papua New Guinea enjoys a relatively benign security environment, but concerns about terrorism have escalated and porous borders continue to permit the spilling over of tensions in neighboring countries as well as illegal trafficking in arms, drugs, and people. With respect to terrorism, toward the end of 2001, in the wake of the September 11 attacks and the subsequent U.S. military action in Afghanistan, the then foreign affairs minister told the National Parliament that there was no real external risk for Papua New Guinea, notwithstanding some instability in the immediate region. Just over a year later, the bombings in Bali, in which more than 180 people (mostly Indonesians and Australians) were killed, caused the incoming foreign affairs minister (and former prime minister), Sir Rabbie Namaliu, to revise this opinion and call for an urgent review of the country's preparedness to deal with a terrorist attack, and of its internal security and intelligence gathering resources.

Prior to this, growing unrest in the neighboring Indonesian province of Papua (formerly Irian Jaya) again underscored the problems of maintaining border security, especially after Indonesia announced its intentions of cracking down on the members of the Papuan Presidium Council who were pushing for a dialogue on autonomy in the province. Then in August 2002, an unidentified group ambushed workers on their way to the Freeport mine in Papua, killing three and injuring eight (mostly Americans). Shortly before this, Papua New Guinea's foreign affairs secretary had told incoming MPs that Papua New Guinea must give priority to border issues, and Foreign Affairs Minister Namaliu had observed that development projects in the border area with Indonesia had come to a standstill due to lack of funding.

In the face of unrest in Papua and requests from Papua activists for support at the Pacific Islands Forum meeting in August 2002, Somare reiterated Papua New Guinea's policy of treating West Papua as an internal matter for Indonesia. The position reflects the nation's interest in good relations with its large western neighbor.

On Papua New Guinea's eastern border, turbulence in the Solomon Islands also has continuing potential to affect Bougainville through cross-border movements. During the Bougainville conflict, the Bougainville Revolutionary Army (BRA) had substantial links with supporters in the Solomon Islands. Early in 2002, there were reports of former BRA fighters involved in shootings in the Solomon Islands' Western Province, where two special constables from the Solomons province of Malaita were killed. Malaitan ex-militants retaliated against Western Province people in the national capital of Honiara. The presence of Bougainvilleans in the Solomon Islands and Solomon Islanders in Bougainville is a concern for authorities in both Honiara and Port Moresby.

Persistent concerns about a growing trade, across the Torres Strait and across the border with Indonesia, in weapons-for-drugs (mostly marijuana) were underlined early in 2002 when a special police operation in the Western Province yielded "a large quantity" of arms and drugs. However, increased surveillance and joint patrolling of the southern border with Australian counterparts has reportedly seen a dramatic decline in illegal activities. The issue of border surveillance has also been a topic of discussion with the New Zealand prime minister. A formal agreement between the National Fisheries Authority and the PNGDF will facilitate an upgrading of fisheries surveillance in Papua New Guinea waters, but the arrival of several illegal immigrants, mostly from Vietnam, in Western Province during 2002 reinforced concerns that Papua New Guinea might be used as a staging point for people-smuggling to Australia and New Zealand.

The border issues are aggravated by the ease in obtaining illegal documentation. In 2001, an investigation was launched into an alleged passport scam within the Department of Foreign Affairs and Trade, and the foreign minister announced a crackdown on abuses of passport, visa, and work-permit procedures. The report of the task force was received in mid- 2002. It implicated a number of foreign affairs officers in illegal activities and recommended a review of migration and citizenship laws and procedures. It was later announced that 18 departmental officers were to be charged with various offenses, with more charges likely. Namaliu also confirmed the government's commitment to removing noncitizens from employment reserved for Papua New Guineans.

Diplomatically, the change of government following the 2002 election is unlikely to bring any substantial change in foreign policy or in Papua New Guinea's perceptions of the external security environment, though Namaliu has spoken of the need to rebuild Papua New Guinea's regional and international standing, which he suggested had been allowed to "drift" under the previous government. He referred specifically to the need for mature, mutually beneficial relations with Australia, New Zealand, Indonesia, Japan, China, and South Korea. Prior to the election, Namaliu had expressed concerns about Papua New Guinea's relationship with Australia slipping back into "colonial era attitudes, or a big brother approach" and suggested that Australia needed to take greater care that it did not convey the impression that it was "taking sides" in Papua New Guinea politics. Later, Somare was quoted as saying he would manage the relationship with Australia differently from his predecessor.

DEFENSE POLICIES AND ISSUES

For a number of years, governments of Papua New Guinea have sought to downsize and restructure the defense forces and rebuild capacity and morale. These goals were set out in a PNGDF white paper in 1999, an inquiry by a ministerial task force in 2000, and the report of a Commonwealth Eminent Persons Group. The Department of Defense conducted an organizational restructure review in 2001, and a new commander was appointed the same year.

Problems persist in carrying through these intentions, however. In a protest against the proposed restructuring, mutinous soldiers and retrenched personnel took control of Moem Barracks in Wewak in early 2002, burning down buildings, raiding the armory, and chasing some officers and their families out of the compound. In a 13-point petition presented to then opposition leader Sir Michael Somare (a resident of Wewak), the soldiers listed, along with industrial demands, calls for the resignation of the prime minister and of the commander of the PNGDF, and several other political demands, including a halt to the privatization of government assets and proposed land mobilization (both included in a World Bank–sponsored structural adjustment program). After unsuccessful negotiations, the Moem Barracks were retaken in a military operation and 24 soldiers were subsequently court-martialed and convicted of civil criminal charges.

In the lead-up to the national elections, a new defense minister was appointed and changes in senior PNGDF positions were announced (though the latter were deferred after a legal challenge). A Defense Intelligence report to the PNGDF commander, Commodore Peter Ilau, suggested that this reshuffling was "election-related" and indicated evidence of a plot to halt the retrenchment exercise and change the current command structure. Amid allegations that the PNGDF was being subjected to "outside [political] influences," it was decided that the PNGDF would not be used in routine operations to assist police in providing security during the 2002 elections. (In 1997, troops had been so used, but some soldiers had been accused of acting in a partisan way, and several had been arrested.) PNGDF personnel were confined to barracks. Notwithstanding this, in June it was reported that some soldiers, as well as the civilian defense secretary, had taken part in the election campaign, and several were later charged with electoral offenses. By year's end, however, some stability seemed to have returned to the military force, and restructuring was under way, with force size down to around 2000 personnel. In a budget brought in by the new government in August, the allocation for defense, against the general trend, was increased from K53.7 million to K64.6 million (US$215,000–US$258,000 at K1 = US$0.25).

CONTRIBUTIONS TO REGIONAL AND GLOBAL SECURITY

Papua New Guinea is an active participant in regional and global forums within the scope of its limited resources, and it has aspirations to engage in peacemaking and peacekeeping in its immediate neighborhood. However, it intends to reduce its role as a processing center for illegal Central and South Asian would-be migrants to Australia.

Papua New Guinea is a signatory to the Treaty of Amity and Cooperation of the Association of Southeast Asian Nations (ASEAN) and a participant in the ASEAN Regional Forum (ARF) and the Asia-Pacific Economic Cooperation (APEC) forum. It is also a prominent member of the Pacific Islands Forum and of the Melanesian Spearhead Group, a regular participant in Commonwealth Heads of Government Meetings (CHOGM), and a member of the joint assembly of the European Union and the African, Caribbean and Pacific Group of States (ACP Group). While its small size and limited financial resources constrain its role in international forums, it has been an outspoken advocate on a number of environmental and humanitarian issues.

Papua New Guinea's defense minister has ruled out the possibility of his country taking part in UN peacekeeping operations, arguing that it does not have the resources. Nevertheless, in September Prime Minister Somare announced that, if wanted, Papua New Guinea is prepared to send police and PNGDF personnel to the Solomon Islands to assist in establishing law and order. Somare also offered to provide financial assistance to the Solomon Islands (following the suspension of a K26 million (US$104,000) grant by the previous government of Papua New Guinea). The backdrop for this proposed assistance was the Pacific Islands Forum meeting in Fiji in August. As well as re-endorsing the earlier Biketawa Declaration on the promotion of democratic governance in the region (see *Asia Pacific Security Outlook 2001*), the forum adopted a further resolution on regional security, supported by Australia. The resolution, the Nasonini Declaration on Regional Security, recognized "the need for immediate and sustained regional action in response to the current regional security environment." Responding to a request from the Solomon Islands prime minister, the final communiqué directed the forum secretariat to mobilize regional action and funds to support the Solomon Islands, where renewed, partly ethnic-based, violence broke out in 2002. Subsequently, Australia, New Zealand, and the United States promised to support the forum in establishing a regional framework for dealing with terrorism.

In midyear, Papua New Guinea officials attended a meeting, hosted by Indonesia in Bali, to discuss security, economic, and cultural cooperation among countries of the Southwest Pacific. The idea of a Southwest Pacific forum was initiated by former Indonesian President Abdurrahman Wahid. Apart from Indonesia and Papua New Guinea, participating countries include Australia, New Zealand, the Philippines, and East Timor.

Papua New Guinea's role as a refugee-/migrant-processing venue began in 2001, when under an agreement with Australia a processing facility was established at the Lombrum naval base in Manus for "boat people" seeking asylum in Australia. The decision remains controversial in both countries. Manus landowners have threatened to close the facility, claiming they have not received promised compensation for land and water, and a breakout by asylum seekers (mostly from Iraq, Iran, and Pakistan) occurred in 2002 in protest over their lengthy detention. As an opposition member of parliament, Somare had been an outspoken critic of the arrangement, and as prime minister he informed Australia that Papua New Guinea would accept no more asylum seekers.

14 Philippines

The Security Environment

President Gloria Macapagal Arroyo calls the central task for the Philippines one of building "a strong republic." The pillars of her political agenda include breaking terrorism, reducing criminality, addressing socioeconomic concerns, and consolidating political institutions. In 2003, the Philippines faces unresolved questions arising from the Muslim secessionist movement in the south, the communist insurgency, and the implications of its vigorous support for the global campaign on anti-terrorism. Its domestic imperatives require the Philippines to give great importance to international cooperation on global terrorism and strengthen its working relationship with the United States. In addition, 2003 will be a highly political year leading up to the 2004 presidential elections.

INTERNAL   The year 2002 ended with the surprise announcement by Arroyo that she will not be a candidate in the May 2004 presidential elections. This came at the culmination of a difficult year for her, involving allegations of corruption in her government, splits in her fragile political coalition, growing opposition from former allies as well as from diehard supporters of deposed president Joseph Estrada, rising crime rates, little sign of real progress in persistent problems of domestic separatism and terrorism, and the continued slow economic growth. In addition, persistent rumors of a coup suggested morale problems in the military, and a call in the Congress for a shift from a presidential to a parliamentary form of government was another source of political pressure.

The official reason for the president's decision not to run again is that she deplores a Philippine penchant for "too much politics." Her decision may help her focus on her political agenda, free from political considerations and charges that her decisions are motivated by reelection ambitions. On the other hand, her lame duck status may undermine her effectiveness.

One of the most pervasive challenges in the Philippines is to strengthen political institutions. As part of the strong republic program, the government convened several summits in 2002 to build more effective cooperation among different governmental agencies and with the broader society. These included summits on kidnapping, political parties, and national intelligence. The political parties summit provided a venue for some members of Congress to propose charter changes related to national police, term limits for elected officials, and new foreign investment provisions.

Despite the summits, leadership problems were evident at many levels, including at the very top as the president herself seemed unable to keep in place and lead a stable cabinet or hold together the broader EDSA 2 coalition that had made her president. In June, Vice President Teofisto Guingona resigned his concurrent position as secretary of foreign affairs, reportedly because of differences with Arroyo over some of the terms of the Philippine-U.S. joint military exercise Balikatan 02-01. A member of an opposition group previously associated with former President Estrada replaced Guingona, causing criticism from civil society organizations. A series of cabinet shake-ups followed in the departments of transportation and communication education, environment and natural resources, agriculture, and the National Economic Development Authority. Illustrative of the disintegrating EDSA 2 coalition, one former cabinet member, Education Secretary Raul Roco, at the end of September became the first former ally to declare a run for the presidency against Arroyo.

The Congress and other institutions were not immune from leadership problems. In the Senate a change of leadership occurring in a dubious manner in June resulted in a standstill as the previous leadership refused to cooperate with the new majority. This was finally resolved after 57 days, but subsequently affected the legislative process as the validity of four passed bills was questioned. A compromise solution was reached approving three bills and requiring the fourth bill on absentee voting to undergo floor deliberation.

There were also leadership problems in the Commission on Elections (COMELEC). This body was compelled to put its house in order, as the

Supreme Court nullified a contract for the implementation of a Voters Registration Identification System project as being over budget. The delay undermined the commission's effectiveness and hindered the conduct of efficient and orderly elections in the country.

Problems related to law and order such as local insurgencies, separatism, criminality, and acts of terrorism continue to preoccupy the country. Police figures showed that violent crimes increased by 25 percent in the first half of 2002 over the same period in the previous year, while robbery and theft were up 40 percent. Allegations of corruption in government led the president to create a Presidential Anti-Graft Commission. In one prominent case, civil society groups filed criminal charges against officials of the Philippine Estates Authority over alleged corruption in constructing the Diosdado Macapagal highway. Other allegations involved the Land Transportation Office, the National Electrification Administration, and the Public Estates Authority. The secretary of justice was accused of taking bribes from one of the members of the House of Representatives, forcing the secretary to take a leave of absence in December.

Military and police operations continue against the New People's Army (NPA), which is the armed wing of the Communist Party of the Philippines (CPP); the Moro Islamic Liberation Front (MILF) insurgency in Mindanao; and the Abu Sayyaf Group (ASG) in the extreme south. The NPA this year intensified its operations against police stations, including kidnapping officials, and, toward the end of the year, it blew up a gigantic bust of former President Ferdinand Marcos. The Philippines has intensified suppression efforts against the CPP/NPA as part of its strong republic agenda, but it is also keeping open lines of communication for peace negotiations as part of a continued strategy combining military and negotiating elements. The government estimates the NPA strength at about 10,000, operating widely around the country. In response to the spate of NPA attacks, the government launched "Operation Gordian Knot," as the most recent in a 30-year history of police and military actions against the NPA. Both the United States and the European Union have condemned the NPA as a terrorist organization.

A peace agreement with the MILF remains on the president's priority list. Negotiations broke off in late 2001, but interim agreements were signed in May 2002. Some lawmakers criticized these agreements for failing to refer to the constitution as their framework. Military action continues. Allegations by the police that several terrorist cells found in

Luzon have links with the MILF may impede the conclusion of a peace agreement. Although the Armed Forces of the Philippines (AFP) over-ran an MILF bomb-training camp in November, the MILF is not labeled as a terrorist organization either by the Philippines or by the United States, apparently out of deference to its ally. This suggests that the government continues to hope that the MILF, estimated to have about 12,000 fighters mostly in Mindanao, can be pulled into negotiations.

In contrast, the government refuses to negotiate with the ASG, gen-erally regarded in Manila as a ragtag group of bandits with no broader aim than to enrich themselves. In 2002, the AFP rousted the ASG from its home base in Basilan, killed ASG leader Abu Sabaya, and captured its chief explosives expert, Abdulmukim Edris. But the ASG stubbornly refuses to disappear. Regrouping in nearby Jolo Island, it remains a serious terrorist threat. At the beginning of 2003, it is apparently still holding seven hostages, four Filipina members of the Jehovah's Wit-nesses, and three Indonesian male sailors. The AFP vows to continue its pursuit of the ASG, possibly with U.S. training support as in the pre-vious "Balikatan" Basilan operation.

While the military action is largely confined to isolated, specific loca-tions around the country, the terrorist groups have increasingly sought to destabilize the country at large through terrorist tactics directed against urban or symbolic targets. In general, these groups do not act in concert with each other, and often they are not internally coordinated. Bombings occurred throughout the past year. A particularly vicious se-ries took place in October 2002, targeting shopping centers, buses and bus terminals, and shrines in the southern part of the country. In re-sponse, the president called on local government officials to participate in police and community anti-terrorism plans. The intelligence com-munity strongly believed that the October attacks were the work of the Southeast Asia–wide Jemaah Islamiah (JI). Earlier this year, two mem-bers of the JI were arrested and jailed for suspected involvement in bomb plots and illegal possession of explosives. When the authorities cap-tured Abdulmukim Edris in a Manila suburb, they found he had con-tacts with JI and was planning attacks on the U.S. embassy and other targets in Manila. The terrorist threat was further underscored to the annoyance of the government when Australia, Canada, and the Euro-pean Union closed their embassies in late November for a time because of what they found to be specific, credible threats to their facilities and personnel.

Increased terrorist activities continue to affect the performance of the Philippine economy. Nevertheless, the economy remains resilient in the face of both terrorism and the economic weakness in major export markets of the United States and Japan. Official figures show that the economy grew by 4.1 percent in the first three quarters of 2002 compared to 3.4 percent in the same period last year. The remittances of overseas Filipinos, estimated conservatively at US$6 billion to US$8 billion a year continues to be a major stimulus to the economy. However, poverty remains high, investment remains weak, unemployment continues to grow, and the government suffers from a large budget deficit. The government has lowered its expectations of gross domestic product growth in 2003 from 5.2 percent to 4.2 percent.

EXTERNAL   The Philippines has substantially strengthened its relations with the United States in the context of its anti-terrorism campaign. In spite of the protests from the left, from January through July 2002, 650 U.S. personnel joined Philippine counterparts in Basilan and Zamboanga in the campaign against the ASG. The U.S. forces were involved in training and engineering work (airfield, access roads, bridges, pumps), while the Philippine forces were engaged in combat roles. The opposition charged that the U.S. troops were actually engaged in combat, and that a U.S. serviceman shot a tribesman in Basilan. Despite such charges, an August survey showed 75 percent of the general public approved of the U.S. presence in the combat zones. There was generally strong local support for the joint effort, which also brought substantial funds into the local economies. The United States provided US$15 million in economic support funds for Mindanao and US$55 million in military assistance.

The defense of Philippine territory in the South China Sea has a lower profile than before. The Philippines participated in drafting an accord that was eventually signed by the Association of Southeast Asian Nations (ASEAN) countries and China at the time of the ASEAN summit meeting in Cambodia in November 2002. Under the accord, the parties promise to refrain from actions that could escalate tensions.

The Philippines supports UN Security Council action against Iraq should Iraq inadequately fulfill its inspections obligations. However, there is concern about how an attack would affect the more than one million Filipino nationals in the Middle East and the Philippine economy. The National Security Council in October 2002 set aside P200 million (US$3.76 million at US$1 = P53.25) for the evacuation of Filipino nationals should hostilities break out and requested oil companies to increase domestic reserves from 12 days to 40 days to lessen the effects of any spike in oil prices.

Defense Policies and Issues

The defense budget for fiscal year 2002 was P60.24 billion (US$1.13 billion) and the Philippine army's share was P15.89 billion (US$298.45 million), the Philippine navy was allocated P6.88 billion (US$129.26 million), and the air force P6.01 billion (US$112.88 million).

Military morale has been a problem. In mid-2002, the Defense Department warned active and retired generals who publicly aired discontent, especially on the issue of the selection of the next chief of staff of the AFP. Frequent leadership change (three AFP chiefs in 2002) is another sore point. The admission in May by the defense secretary that the military had facilitated the payment of ransom in a June 2001 incident in Basilan also affected morale.

Bilateral military-to-military ties with the United States are regarded by the government as important to strengthening the country's own military capabilities and as a contribution to the broader struggle against terrorism. Increased cooperation with the United States on anti-terrorism includes not just the continuing joint Balikatan exercises, but also the signing in November 2002 of a five-year Mutual Logistics Support Agreement (MLSA). The agreement allows the United States to establish storage centers for supplies, support services, and medical services, thus permitting the Philippines to become a supply center for anti-terrorist operations. Other cooperative efforts may take place in humanitarian assistance, disaster relief, rescue operations, and maritime anti-pollution, either with the Philippines or elsewhere. Opponents criticize the agreement as inviting U.S. bases back into the Philippines, a charge the government hotly denies. Critics also argue that the agreement was improperly treated as an executive agreement not requiring Senate review.

Contributions to Regional and Global Security

The Philippines contributes to regional and global security primarily through its engagement in ASEAN and in the United Nations. A series of bilateral agreements, as part of a network of international cooperative defense accords, also help strengthen the regional order. Philippine efforts internationally as well as domestically have a strong focus on anti-terrorism. The country continues to attach importance to economic cooperation activities as well.

In recognition of the increasing threat of terrorism, the Philippines, Indonesia, and Malaysia signed the Agreement on Information Exchange and Establishment of Communication Procedures to fight terrorism and transnational crime in the region. After the October 2002 Bali bombings, the president asked that the joint monitoring committee be convened under the agreement. The Philippines has defense agreements with five other ASEAN member-states covering such items as exchanges of defense personnel, information and intelligence exchanges, and research and development of defense products. In July this year, the Philippines and Malaysia held their annual small-scale joint military exercise in northern Luzon involving mostly classroom activities.

The Philippines is also discussing a bilateral anti-terrorism agreement with Australia that may include joint operational and training activities, and another agreement with Germany.

The government also affirmed its commitment to the global war against terrorism and its support for the UN Security Council Resolutions on states aiding terrorism and the dismantling of weapons of mass destruction. The Philippine National Security Council has approved extending political, security, and humanitarian assistance to the United States should it attack Iraq with the backing of the UN Security Council, and if the extension is consistent with the country's national interest and in accordance with the constitution.

In a speech at Japan's Waseda University in May, President Arroyo unveiled a proposal that the ASEAN Regional Forum (ARF) "move beyond confidence building and advance into preventive diplomacy and conflict resolution." She suggested that in this manner the region take a more comprehensive approach to the problem of weak or failing states that become the breeding ground or refuge of terrorists.

In view of the development gaps in the country, the Philippines is seeking to revive interest in the Brunei-Indonesia-Malaysia-Philippines East ASEAN Growth Area (BIMP-EAGA), a program to promote mutually beneficial cooperation in the adjacent areas of these countries. Concomitant with this revival is the signing of a bilateral agreement with Indonesia on fisheries in January. The agreement calls for a joint Philippine-Indonesian management plan for tuna fisheries in the Celebes and Sulawesi seas and defines the total allowable catch in the Indonesian Exclusive Economic Zone (EEZ).

15 Russia

THE SECURITY ENVIRONMENT

INTERNAL   In 2003–2004, Russia holds legislative and presidential elections, faces a peak in its international debt repayments, and continues to grapple with a series of difficult internal security and defense policy challenges, including the still potent Chechnyan threat and the on-going deterioration of its defense organization. Nevertheless, the outlook is for continuation and further consolidation of the "Putin stability" that succeeded the chaotic Yeltsin period.

In December 2003, Russians will cast votes for 450 seats in the Duma, and presidential elections will take place in March 2004. Unlike previous election cycles since the breakup of the Soviet Union, the results appear fairly predictable. The still very popular Vladimir Putin is universally expected to run, and win, and the United Russia Party his administration supports is likely to do well in the Duma. The next parliament will contain fewer political groupings. Next to United Russia, the communists are certain to be represented by a major faction. The liberals, the Union of Right Forces and Yabloko, will need to try harder, while the fate of the ultranationalists hangs in the balance, to be decided largely by whether Putin still feels a need for them.

The Kremlin (that is the Putin administration) is a coalition of the old Yeltsin "family," new "oligarchs," active and retired security officers ("checkists," many of them from Putin's native St. Petersburg), and liberal economic reformers. The balance of power and influence among them is constantly being tested, but the coalition is unlikely to unravel before the elections. Though Putin faces little organized opposition, he has consistently continued his efforts to centralize political power—both at the national and regional levels—and tighten the government's grip on the media. He has largely succeeded in these objectives.

Like the rest of the country, the Far East and Siberia are more tightly controlled by the Kremlin. The change of Yakutia's president and Primorie's governor in 2001 brought to office figures more congenial to Moscow. In 2002, a multimillionaire member of the old Yeltsin "family" took over Chukotka, and a young, new-generation oligarch, Alexander Khloponin, won in Krasnoyarsk to succeed the controversial General Alexander Lebed, who was killed in an air crash. Some analysts see Khloponin as having the makings of a post-Putin presidential candidate.

Economic issues will dominate the upcoming elections and generally reinforce the Kremlin's position. Russia's economy continues to grow, but at a fairly moderate rate of about 4 percent annually. This is well below the 8 percent that Putin has said is indispensable for a true economic takeoff, but it is an improvement over the earlier post-Soviet period, and Russia's cities have become more livable. Investment continues to be low, and the state remains a heavy burden on the economy. However, after massive reforms in 2000–2002, further economic transformation will be put on hold until after the elections.

For several years now, the Russian leadership had awaited 2003 with fear. Russia is scheduled to pay a record US$17.9 billion to its foreign creditors in principal and interest (compared to US$14 billion in 2002). However, high oil prices since 1999 have allowed the Russian government to create an appreciable currency reserve to be able to survive the debt repayment peak. The fiscal year 2003 federal budget is projected to be in surplus, for the third consecutive year. The expected 4 percent growth (in exchange rate terms) will bring the gross domestic product to US$414 billion, allowing the federal government to spend the equivalent of US$73 billion. Of this, US$10.9 billion (or roughly three times as much in purchasing power parity [PPP] terms) will go toward national defense.

Under Putin, spending on national defense and law enforcement has been rising steadily. In fiscal 2003, it will reach 34.7 percent in the federal budget compared with 31.5 percent the previous year. In current ruble terms, defense expenditures alone have quadrupled in the four years from 1999 through 2003. This is partly due to the 14 percent per annum inflation, partly to the war in Chechnya, and in large measure to attempts to address the abominably low living standards of Russian servicemen.

Despite many official claims to the contrary, fighting in Chechnya continues. The rebels enjoy a wide freedom of maneuver and strike almost at will at the Russian forces and Moscow-loyal Chechens. In a spectacular attack in August 2002, they brought down a military transport helicopter, killing 120 people (more than died in the Kursk submarine disaster in 2000). Even more traumatic was the October seizure of a Moscow theater, resulting in the deaths of all the Chechen hostage takers and about 130 hostages. This was not the largest death toll from terrorism in Russia's recent history, but it occurred in the capital, visibly reminding the political elite that they were not immune from the effects of the continuing warfare. In December 2002, the pro-Moscow Chechen government headquarters in Grozny was annihilated by suicide bombers.

Despite the lack of success, the Kremlin firmly adheres to a strategy of pacification by means of military suppression and financial assistance, and flatly refuses to negotiate with "terrorists." It hopes that a referendum on a new constitution will give legitimacy to the pro-Moscow administration. The situation is at an impasse, with the guerillas unable to dislodge the Russian forces and the latter unable to fully control the province. In the early aftermath, the Moscow theater attack strengthened support from an angry public for a hard-line approach. Although there are few signs that Chechnya might become a major electoral issue in 2003–2004, over the longer term the continuing costs of the war and policy failures of his administration may yet prove to be Putin's Achilles' heel.

Apart from Chechnya, which is officially dubbed an "anti-terrorist operation," there have not been major cases of terrorism involving Russia. The crime scene is still very lively, complete with assassinations and bombings, but most incidents, including the killing in 2002 of the governor of Magadan, are economically motivated and do not threaten the government's stability. Racism and xenophobia have meanwhile become permanent features, especially in the large metropolitan areas. The former is mainly directed against Asians and blacks, and the latter against economic migrants from the Moslem republics of the former USSR. The riots in Moscow following Russia's World Soccer Cup loss to Japan in August 2002 shook both the authorities and the public. Another less visible threat to Russian society over the longer term comes from the growth of HIV-AIDS, which international organizations have warned could reach epidemic proportions in coming years.

EXTERNAL   In Russian foreign policy, new agenda items are slowly moving the cold war off the center stage. Neither the World Trade Organization (WTO) accession nor the North Atlantic Treaty Organization (NATO) and the European Union (EU) enlargements align the elites along the competitive lines of openness and protectionism.

All the differences concerning the Middle East and other issues notwithstanding, Moscow has consolidated a new relationship with Washington. While it is not exactly the strategic partnership that was widely touted in the aftermath of the terrorist attacks in the United States on September 11, 2001, it is certainly much friendlier and virtually safe from international crises or traditional arms issues. From the Russian side, pragmatic economic and political interests rather than ideology or rivalry for leadership underlie this relationship. For Putin, unlike his many predecessors, America's might, in and of itself, is not a threat and perhaps not even a problem. It is a fact of life. Despite its clear preference for a negotiated solution to the Iraq problem, Moscow decided in advance not to oppose Washington's use of force against Baghdad. Russia can also be expected to play a role in a post-Saddam settlement, in an attempt to rescue some of its commercial and financial interests in Iraq.

In relations with the European Union, the enlargement of which will advance its territory to the borders of the Commonwealth of Independent States (CIS), economic issues clearly dominate. The medium-to-long-term issue (after Russia joins the WTO, which is unlikely before 2005 and possibly 2007) is to create a free trade area between Russia and the European Union.

In the wake of September 11, Moscow has realized that its oil and gas resources and the new friendliness with the West are empowering it to play a big role in the field of energy diplomacy. Russia presents itself as a reliable supplier of hydrocarbons to all its principal partners. Energy diplomacy also in part underlies Russia's relations with the CIS countries. In an important foreign policy success, Moscow resolved problems over the delimitation of the oil- and gas-rich Caspian Sea with both of its neighbors there, Kazakhstan and Azerbaijan. However, in other cases, notably in Central Asia and the Caucasus, traditional security considerations still prevail. In September 2002, Putin personally served an ultimatum to the Georgian government to cooperate with Russia in isolating Chechen rebels and terrorists or face Russia's unilateral action in its territory. This incident, in which Georgia ultimately complied, demonstrates Moscow's willingness to emulate U.S. policy on a regional scale.

Russia continues to regard the Asia Pacific region as important. Ever since he stood in for Yeltsin in 1999, Putin has been attending the meetings of the Asia-Pacific Economic Cooperation (APEC) leaders, missing only the October 2002 meeting because of the terrorist incident in Moscow. Aside from symbolizing Russia's commitment to the region and helping Putin increase his stature on the world stage, his attendance has also served to focus the Russian government bureaucracy on subjects related to the Asia Pacific region.

Russia's Asia policy, however, begins at home. In an effort to spur the implementation of the faltering regional development programs, Putin in 2002 made a weeklong trip to the Russian Far East and Siberia. Since then, these areas, long neglected by high-level Moscow officials, have hosted other high-ranking officials, including National Security Council Secretary Vladimir Rushaylo.

Top Russian energy companies have also started to pay more attention to the Asian markets. Gazprom expects Asia to become as important as Europe in its export strategy by 2015–2020. Yukos is lobbying hard for an oil pipeline to run from East Siberia to Daqing, China, whereas another company, Transneft, proposes to run it to Nakhodka, on the Sea of Japan. The several Sakhalin oil projects represent the largest foreign investments in Russia. Plans are being made to supply oil to the U.S. and Japanese markets.

Beyond energy, there is hardly an Asia-wide Russian policy. Interested political figures and the foreign and security policy bureaucracies continue to think in bilateral terms. China has priority.

Russo-Chinese relations have been undergoing an important modification since September 11. Using China to balance the United States has ceased to be one of the reasons and objectives for Moscow's cooperation with Beijing. Putin has clearly shown he is no longer interested in Russia playing the world's premier critic of U.S. policies, providing cover for others, including China. Although Beijing must have been shaken by Putin's quick abandonment of Russia's opposition to the U.S. withdrawal from the Anti-Ballistic Missile (ABM) treaty, this has not harmed Sino-Russian relations. In general, Russo-Chinese relations remain stable and positive.

For its part, Moscow values Beijing's stabilizing role in Central Asia (via the Shanghai Cooperation Organization [SCO]) and in Korea—two areas of great importance to Russia. After a period of stagnation at around US$7 billion per year, there are indications that Russo-Chinese trade will continue to grow—it has already reached some US$12 billion. Of this, US$1 billion–US$2 billion is Russia's export of military hardware and technology.

Relations with Japan, potentially Russia's leading partner in its modernization, are slowly emerging from stagnation. Since the fruitless Putin-Mori 2001 summit in Irkutsk, Tokyo has been preoccupied with domestic issues, which left little time for foreign policy initiatives. The influential group in the Japanese establishment seeking to promote understanding with Russia had become discredited. In Russia, the high pitch of the debate on sovereignty issues related to Kaliningrad transit leaves little hope for an early change of policy on the South Kuriles. Still, the resumption of summit-level dialogue in January 2003 in Moscow offers a chance for gradually constructing the basis for a new Russo-Japanese relationship.

India traditionally enjoys a reputation in Moscow of being a co-operative partner. But it is now being taken more seriously following New Delhi's refusal of Putin's offer to mediate between India and Pakistan. While the Russians are generally sympathetic to India in its fight against terror-prone secessionists and draw broad parallels between Kashmir and Chechnya, they are increasingly concerned about strategic stability in South Asia. Clearly, the current basis of Russia's "excellent" relations with India (arms sales) is too narrow. The Russians see a need to expand and deepen their ties to India, whose importance for the region and value to Russia's Asia policy are likely to grow over time.

Relations with Seoul have remained stable and friendly. Russia pins high hopes on the inter-Korean dialogue that, if successful, could yield substantial economic benefits for Moscow. Should the two Koreas develop an effective railway link, this would open a new "land bridge" option from Pusan to St. Petersburg, connecting Northeast Asia to Western Europe across the Russian territory. In particular, the Russian government hopes that the transit route would help develop the backward Far Eastern provinces.

To gain additional leverage in the South, as well as to positively influence the North, Moscow has intensified its contacts with Pyongyang. By helping Kim Jong Il out of isolation, Putin hopes (besides promoting Russia's economic interests) to defuse tensions on the Korean peninsula, avoid the abrupt collapse of the world's last Stalinist regime, and to gain additional currency in relations with the United States and Japan. Still, Putin has to concede two things: (1) that Kim prefers no intermediaries in his difficult dialogue with the United States, and (2) that Washington may take issue with Russia's too close ties with the confessed proliferator of nuclear arms and peddler of missile technology. The precipitous downward spiral of Pyongyang-Washington relations in the later part of 2002 placed Russian diplomacy in a difficult position.

Apart from its immediate neighborhood, Russia remains a peripheral player in much of Asia. Its relations with ASEAN countries have been continuing on a fairly moderate level. The only notable exception is Vietnam, where Moscow has been trying to use the personal connections built during the 1950s–1980s to promote closer economic cooperation.

DEFENSE POLICIES AND ISSUES

Russia's defense policy is increasingly responding to new challenges, even as its underlying philosophy, defense planning, and current defense posture remain rooted in the cold war. Russia has abandoned strategic nuclear rivalry and is learning to live with U.S. forces deployed in Central Asia, American advisers in Georgia, and a forthcoming full membership for the Baltic nations in NATO.

Even as the Russian military organization continues in crisis (as evidenced by frequent desertions from the ranks, barracks shootings, and arms depot explosions), calls for terminating conscription and introducing the principle of an all-volunteer force (AVS) are growing louder. The Union of Right Forces has succeeded in persuading Putin to take a closer look at their military reform proposal that is built around an AVS concept. The largely conservative military establishment resists such a radical reform (and the Ministry of Defense leadership is largely passive), but the abolition of the draft is dictated both by the dwindling demographic resource base and the mood of the electorate. Putin cannot afford to ignore either, but he is equally loath to alienate the top brass in the election cycle. This means that the phasing out of conscription is unlikely to be speeded up.

Russian defense exports continue to dwarf domestic defense orders, in 2002 by about 2 to 1. Of these exports, four-fifths are sent to China and India, in roughly equal proportions. Whole defense enterprises survive thanks to New Delhi (Irkutsk) or Beijing (Komsomolsk). Conventional defense cooperation with India is virtually unrestricted, and the restrictions on China sales are being eased. These sales have helped buy time for the needed consolidation of Russia's large and inefficient defense industry, but this politically difficult issue remains high on the economic and security agendas. In the meantime, defense and dual-use exports remain an actual and potential source of tension with the West, with considerable scope to flare up depending on the security relations of the United States with China, Iran, and other Russian customers.

CONTRIBUTIONS TO REGIONAL AND GLOBAL SECURITY

Russia remains committed to nuclear arms reductions. Under the 2002 treaty with the United States on strategic arsenals, it is obligated to cut its stockpiles to 2,000 weapons. The Russian leadership has not yet exercised its "option" of responding to the U.S. missile defense program. Indeed, Russia has repeatedly expressed interest in participating in such a program with the United States and its NATO allies.

Inadequate funding remains a major problem in implementing disarmament obligations and pledges (e.g., utilizing nuclear submarines or eliminating chemical weapons stocks). To help Russia, Group of Seven (G7) nations agreed in 2002 to US$20 billion in grants over ten years. The United States, which funds half this program, is also offering funds to help Russia destroy its cold war arsenals.

From 2002, Russia and NATO have decided to upgrade and deepen their relationship through the newly created council in which Russia in theory has an equal voice with its NATO partners. The new body concentrates on countering international terrorism, proliferation of weapons of mass destruction (WMD), missile defense, peacekeeping, and military reform. Major sustained efforts, however, will be needed to overcome the remaining vestiges of the cold war and securely embed Russia within the Western security community.

Meanwhile, Russia is engaged in building security institutions in Central Asia. It proposed that the 1992 Collective Security Treaty with Kazakhstan, the Kyrgyz Republic, Tajikistan, Armenia, and Belarus be redesigned to become a regional security organization. In particular, Moscow is adding an air force element to its predominantly army/ border guards military presence in the region. In a parallel effort, Moscow is cooperating with Beijing and Central Asian capitals (minus Ashgabat) in making the SCO a vehicle for stability and regional development. Apart from tolerating U.S. and other Western presence in

Central Asia and generally cooperating with them in Afghanistan, Russia has yet to explore the potential for closer cooperation with Western powers and their militaries in this volatile region.

Russia has joined the United States and other nuclear powers in efforts to alleviate tensions between India and Pakistan. This informal concert, based on common vital interests, is likely to continue in case of future complications between the two countries. To defuse the crisis provoked by Pyongyang's withdrawal from the Framework Accord, Moscow proposed jointly guaranteeing, with Beijing, American nuclear assurances to North Korea.

16 Singapore

As Southeast Asia grapples with terrorism, Singapore faces a more uncertain, fluid, and complex security environment. More than other countries in the region, Singapore, a small island-state, is feeling intensely vulnerable because its lifeline is inextricably tied to the external environment. Open air- and sea-corridors of communications are essential to its survival and prosperity. Its exposure of a terrorist plot, involving local and regional members of the al Qaeda–linked Jemaah Islamiah (JI) terrorist group, highlighted Singapore as a target of radical Muslims, both as an integral node of the U.S.-led global economy and as a logistic base for the U.S. military presence in the Pacific and Indian oceans. Other than global terrorism, the spectrum of potential threats to Singapore's national security has widened to include transnational organized crime, piracy, and illegal immigration; all of these factors pose challenges, especially in the near term. As these transnational threats require transnational responses, Singaporeans worry whether a sufficient international consensus will be developed around the issues and, if so, whether the other needed partners have the political will and capacity to deal with them effectively.

INTERNAL   Terrorism and the economy dominate Singaporean concerns about domestic security. Singaporeans have been shaken by the arrests in December 2001 and August 2002 of 36 persons implicated in a plot to unify the Islamic militant groups and foment communal unrest in the region. Thirty-two of the detainees were allegedly members of JI, an Indonesia-based terrorist network with the goal of forcibly

145

establishing a pan-Southeast Asian Islamic State, or Daulah Islamiyah Nusantara. While it was reassuring that the Internal Security Department had disrupted JI's plan to bomb targets in Singapore, the details also demonstrated the ease with which Southeast Asian radicals crossed borders and acquired and moved explosive materials, and the extent of their connections with international networks. Some of the JI members had received tactical and weapons training at al Qaeda camps in Afghanistan, as well as weapons training with the Moro Islamic Liberation Front in the Philippines, while several others gained combat experience in Maluku and Batam Island in Indonesia. Highly cognizant of the divisive power of religion and ethnicity in the Muslim-dominated region, Singapore is gravely concerned about the growth of transnational Islamic radical groups and their potential to provoke unrest in neighboring countries.

Identification of the JI network in Singapore caused domestic soul-searching over how well integrated the Muslim Malay community—about 15 percent of the city-state's population—is in the Singaporean mainstream. In October 2002, 123 Muslim organizations in Singapore issued a joint statement denouncing those who justify terrorism in the name of Islam. Muslim leaders supported the government's white paper on the JI, released in January 2003, which contained several recommendations to counter the threat of the terrorist network.

The discovery of Southeast Asian terrorist networks, weak economies in the region, and the general slump in the global economy have severely affected Singapore's highly internationalized economy. Nonetheless, Singapore has weathered the economic slump well. The World Investment Report 2002 by the United Nations Conference on Trade and Development (UNCTAD) ranked Singapore as fifth in attracting foreign direct investment in 2001; Singapore recorded a 59 percent increase over the previous year to US$9 billion for the first increase since 1998. Singapore's focus on biomedical sciences and the government's pro-investment incentives help explain this improved performance. Real gross domestic product grew at 2.2 percent in 2002, while the 2003 outlook varies from 2 percent to as much as 5 percent depending upon estimates of external demand. The wide variance in estimates illustrates the uncertainties in this year's political and security environment.

The government established an Economic Review Committee in October 2001 to develop future economic development strategies, and it is particularly looking to strengthen ties with China and India so as to broaden Singapore's economic base. Singapore continues also to actively develop its bilateral free trade arrangements, successfully negotiating agreements with Japan and the United States.

Politically, the position of the ruling People's Action Party (PAP) remains impregnable. In the November 2001 election, which took place during the worst recession since independence, the party not only retained all its seats (82 out of 84), but also significantly increased its share of the popular vote in the 29 contested constituencies by about 10 percentage points to 75.3 percent. The desire of the electorate to rally around its political leadership during harder times and its confidence in the PAP's economic leadership may help explain these results.

Popular Prime Minister Goh Chok Tong has indicated that he would step down before the next general election, scheduled for 2007. His deputy, Lee Hsien Loong, is expected to succeed and continue the PAP tradition of smooth leadership transitions.

EXTERNAL   To Singaporeans, the geopolitical environment in Southeast Asia continues to look less stable and predictable than in the previous two decades. The outlook in Indonesia is particularly troubling as the country is suffering from a prolonged economic downturn made worse by an indecisive government preoccupied with political infighting and the 2004 presidential elections. The bombings in Bali in October 2002 added to Indonesia's economic woes and augmented concerns about the security of the sprawling archipelago, which has spawned a rash of Islamic radical groups after the fall of Suharto. Singapore, Malaysia, and the Philippines have acted swiftly against terrorism. But the region's overall reputation for safety and stability depend on similar action in Indonesia.

Indonesia's initial denials and inaction in the face of intelligence pointing to its role as a center of Southeast Asian terrorism has been an irritant in Singaporean-Indonesian relations. JI spiritual leader Abu Bakar Bashir, an Indonesian cleric, was commonly believed in Singapore to be involved in the plot to attack Singapore targets. His arrest and the Indonesian police's successful pursuit and arrest of several participants in the Bali bombings are regarded as hopeful signs, but there is still concern that Indonesia lacks the fully trained intelligence and police forces and the political will to carry out an effective crackdown on militants threatening the entire region.

Indonesia is also a principal source of piracy that has traditionally plagued the heavily trafficked shipping routes in the Singapore Strait and the Strait of Malacca. Security forces in Singapore are concerned that with international terrorism, piracy could escalate to a more virulent form that would destroy shipping facilities and block shipping channels.

Concerning Malaysia, there is also a new uncertainty about Malaysian politics following Prime Minister Mahathir bin Mohammed's sudden announcement that he will retire from office in October 2003, one year ahead of the general elections in 2004. As a result, some in Singapore fear that bilateral relations will take a beating, if in a more competitive political environment Malaysian politicians resort to the tactic of appealing to Malaysian nationalism by castigating Singapore as a threat.

The outstanding bilateral issues between the two countries, such as the water supply contract, Malaysian passport controls in the Tanjong Pagar railway station, and a disputed islet, continue to irritate relations. While such issues complicate the relationship with Malaysia, Singapore values the strong anti-terrorist approach of the Malaysian government and its stable economy. Even at the height of the dispute between the two countries over the outstanding issues in January 2002, amid talk of war in the Malaysian media, Singapore's Foreign Minister S. Jayakumar took pains to stress that the two countries' common bilateral interests exceed their differences.

There is disappointment that the Association of Southeast Asian Nations (ASEAN) has been largely ineffective in tackling the economic and security challenges confronting the region, issuing obscure policy pronouncements when articulate action is required. The region's defense establishments still have some way to go to build the kind of connections and trust needed to fight new threats like terrorism. The development of the 23-member ASEAN Regional Forum (ARF) is so gradual and protocol-bound that it risks being outpaced by a new security forum, the Asia Security Conference, organized by the London-based International Institute of Strategic Studies (IISS) and referred to in Singapore as the "Shangri-La Dialogue." The Shangri-La Dialogue brought together ministers and security officials from 18 countries to exchange views on Asia Pacific security challenges, including terrorism, cross-Strait relations, and weapons nonproliferation. The participants also addressed tensions in South Asia between Pakistan and India. Plans are afoot for a second conference in Singapore this year, again organized by the IISS.

The Singapore government believes that multilateral meetings, such as the ARF and the Asia Security Conference, are important for promoting dialogue among countries with a stake in the region's security. It holds the view that these forums are valuable for encouraging greater transparency and inculcating habits of cooperation between the defense and military establishments.

Beyond Southeast Asia, relations between China, Japan, and the United States are regarded as the most important set of relationships for East Asian security. Singapore seeks good ties with all of them. With the United States in particular, Singapore enjoys strong economic ties and a close defense relationship. The joint memorandum allowing U.S. forces access to military facilities in Singapore dates from 1990, with a 1998 addendum allowing U.S. navy ships and aircraft carriers to berth at Changi Naval Base. The risk for Singapore, however, is that its association with the U. S. government and U.S. businesses in Singapore may make the city a target of radical Islamic terrorists angry at U.S. policy in the Middle East and elsewhere. The JI plan to blow up the U.S. and Israeli embassies in Singapore illustrates this threat.

Singapore also actively engages other powers that have a stake in regional stability. These include India and France and Singapore's partners in the Five Power Defense Arrangements (FPDA; Australia, Malaysia, New Zealand, and the United Kingdom).

DEFENSE POLICIES AND ISSUES

The development of conventional military capabilities remains the key focus of Singapore defense policy. However, the near-term unconventional threats posed by terrorism, transnational organized crime, piracy, and illegal immigration require comprehensive approaches combining traditional defense, intelligence, political, and socioeconomic strategies.

After September 11, 2001, the city-state immediately tightened the coordination between the Ministry of Defense (MINDEF), the Singapore Armed Forces (SAF), the Ministry of Home Affairs, and other home-front agencies. The intent is to better monitor threat situations, preempt attacks, and respond swiftly and effectively should prevention fail. At the ministerial level, this effort is driven by the Security Policy Review Committee (SPRC), chaired by Deputy Prime Minister and Minister for Defense Tony Tan. The SPRC is assisted by the National Security Secretariat (NSS), which coordinates the efforts of various security and intelligence agencies and engages in developmental planning to ensure that the necessary capabilities will meet the threats.

Singapore has also set up a Joint Counter-Terrorism Centre (JCTC) to integrate Singapore's multi-agency intelligence efforts and serve as a point of contact for international counter-terrorism cooperation. The National Security Task Force was also established in 2002 to maintain an overview of the national picture and coordinate and facilitate the optimal deployment of national capabilities and resources. A new Immigration Checkpoints Authority has been set up to bring customs enforcement officers under one authority with the Ministry of Home Affairs and strengthen checks at all border entry points.

Ever vigilant, Singapore has been preparing itself for a variety of contingencies, including low-intensity conflict and attacks aimed at disrupting social or economic life, or aimed at intimidating the country and destroying its national will. The threat can come in different forms—physical or cyber attack, unsophisticated weapons, or weapons of mass destruction. Legislation has also been enacted to control the transit of 600 strategic items, such as chemicals, viruses, and computer software, which can be used to make nuclear, biological, and chemical weapons. The enhanced export control regime is also a reflection of Singapore's commitment to international non-proliferation of weapons of mass destruction.

To respond to these diverse challenges, the Singaporean authorities work closely with counterparts in neighboring friendly countries to promote peace and stability in the region and beyond. It is recognized that the fight against global terrorism must be pursued at the regional and international levels to be effective and credible. Since September 11, Singapore has increased cooperation with foreign intelligence and law enforcement agencies.

DEFENSE SPENDING AND R&D   The defense budget for 2003 will be greater than the US$8.2 billion allotted for 2002, underscoring the national importance placed on countering terrorism threats. Much of the increase in spending will be on counter-terrorism measures, although there will be no letup in upgrading the conventional warfare capabilities of the SAF.

Singapore has an integrated fighting force of 50,000, made up of regulars and conscripts. Another 300,000 are "Operationally Ready National Servicemen." The country seeks to compensate for its tight manpower and space constraints with sophisticated defense weapons and technology and quality training, including training in overseas facilities. Singapore also commits the financial resources needed for such a force, spending up to 6 percent of its gross domestic product on defense, a far higher percentage than other advanced countries. Four percent of the defense budget goes into research and development. MINDEF's Defense Science and Technology Agency (DSTA) is, along with SAF's highly educated personnel and a versatile local defense industry, one of three key pillars underpinning Singapore's ability to harness technology for defense purposes.

In this manner, Singapore has built a strong indigenous defense technology capability over the years, tailored to its specific environment and needs. It has now gone further with defense technology, focusing on developing both individual and organizational abilities to absorb new concepts, technologies, and capabilities. These include the SAF's exploration information networks and remotely operated platforms and precision weapons that will revolutionize defense operations in the future.

An important element in the SAF's transformation process is the nurturing of a generation of technology-savvy and capable military leadership with a clear understanding of how to integrate sophisticated systems and equipment. Singaporean officers with engineering or technical backgrounds are required to go through a six-month diploma course in defense technology before they attend the command and staff course. Those without technical backgrounds attend a month-long military technology program. This focus on mastering technology extends also to all soldiers, sailors, and airmen who are also trained to operate and maintain various high-tech systems in the field.

Because of space limitations, the Singapore government cooperates with other governments in training programs. In July 2002, the Republic of Singapore Air Force (RSAF) opened new pilot training facilities in France, where 49 fighter pilots are training. The navy successfully test-fired the Barak anti-missile defense system in an exercise in the South China Sea.

PROCUREMENT   Because of its geostrategic importance and the endemic instability in the region, Singapore has undertaken a program to modernize and upgrade its naval and air forces so as to enhance their abilities to effectively patrol the Singapore Strait and the Strait of Malacca, and to maintain their sophisticated defense capabilities. Singapore has the most advanced air warfare capability in Southeast Asia. Its air force is first in the region to purchase the Apache attack helicopters equipped with Longbow radar, a significant force multiplier that will further boost Singapore as the region's most potent air force. It took delivery of the first of 20 Apache attack helicopters in May 2002 in the United States. The RSAF's A-4 SU Super Skyhawks will be replaced over the next three to six years. Contenders include Typhoon by Eurofighter, the Russian Sukhoi, Dassault's Rafale and F-16 Block 60 Fighting Falcon, the F/A -18 E/F Hornet, and the F-15 Eagle.

In August 2002, the navy's second submarine, the *RSS Chieftain*, became fully operational, enhancing the navy's anti-submarine warfare capability. Two more submarines will arrive from Sweden in 2004.

Facilities continue to be improved. By 2004, fighter aircrafts will be able to take off from Changi when the new air force facilities are completed at the Changi East Complex. This will give the RSAF greater flexibility to disperse its assets while, at the same time, allow it to better maximize the limited local training airspace. The RSAF now has fighter planes at Tengah and Paya Lebar air bases. The Changi East site will be the third to house these aircraft. A fourth air base in Sembawang is used mainly for helicopter operations. Another improvement to the air force's operational readiness is its ability now to refuel all of its fighter jets in midair, thus increasing their reach. In July 2002, the RSAF transferred six trainer aircraft to its Indonesian counterpart, and was expected to deliver another 13 by the end of 2002. The Indonesian Air Force accepted Singapore's offer of its decommissioned SF-260 SIAI-Marchetti fleet in 2002.

CONTRIBUTIONS TO REGIONAL AND GLOBAL SECURITY

At the multilateral level, Singapore contributes to regional defense and security cooperation in the region by seeking to strengthen multilateral arrangements such as the FPDA and the ARF. To ensure maritime safety, the Indonesian and Singapore navies have conducted coordinated patrols to combat piracy, which is a significant threat to maritime traffic along the sea lanes passing through the region. The SAF is also actively engaged in multilateral defense cooperation and confidence-building measures through its participation in multilateral exercises, such as the Western Pacific Mine Countermeasure Exercise and Western Pacific Diving Exercise hosted by the Republic of Singapore Navy last year— the largest multilateral mine-clearing exercise in the Singapore Strait.

The SAF has also played an active role in developing several multilateral programs designed to promote confidence building among regional forces, such as the inaugural Pacific Armies Chiefs Conference in Singapore in 1999 and the Milleninum Air Power Conference in 2000, which provided a forum for air force chiefs around the world to discuss developments in air-power concepts and technology.

Singapore also plays an active part in supporting the UN Charter. It is an elected non-permanent member of the UN Security Council, and was the president of the Council in January 2001 and March 2002. It is also an elected member of the UN Commission on International Trade Law and the Governing Council of the International Maritime Organization.

Although the SAF is small and largely made up of citizen soldiers, it has contributed to UN peacekeeping, peacemaking, and arms inspection missions in various countries over the years. At the end of October 2002, the SAF deployed a company of 160 combat peacekeepers and a helicopter detachment to the UN Mission of Support in East Timor (UNMISET). The force commander for UNMISET is an SAF officer.

17 Thailand

The Security Environment

INTERNAL   Prime Minister Thaksin Shinawatra's second year in office has been characterized by a strong internal political agenda, aimed to consolidate his political power base and ensure his longer-term political survival. Having successfully dodged dismissal during his first term, on account of his non-disclosure of assets prior to becoming prime minister, Thaksin has moved aggressively on the internal scene to strengthen his ruling coalition and suppress potential sources of opposition. This effort has generated resistance and criticism within some largely urban circles, but the prime minister's political position in 2003 looks unassailable. While Thai politics can take unanticipated turns, the prime minister is in a strong position to complete the remainder of his term, which goes until January 2005, and he expects to win a second term. This would be unprecedented in Thailand's democratic history.

During his second year, Thaksin's influence increased most visibly in the National Assembly, but it also stretched to the Thai military and the press. In January 2002, the prime minister announced that the New Aspiration Party (NAP) and the Chart Pattana Party (CPP) would merge with his Thai Rak Thai (TRT) Party, meaning "Thais Love Thais." Since the CPP had been an opposition party, this moved another block of parliamentary ministers into the ruling camp and resulted in a more than two-thirds majority for the governing coalition in the 500-member National Assembly. This is an unprecedented position for any Thai prime minister, theoretically giving the government the votes to amend the Constitution. However, the coalition is less united than it may appear as the merger increased the number of diverse factions in the ruling group, potentially destabilizing the TRT, and the threads uniting these factions are based more on political expediency than on some unity of idea or purpose. The opposition remains vocal and has brought impeachment charges against nine ministers, but faces a significant leadership transition as former Prime Minister Chuan Leekpai, leader of the main opposition Democrat Party, retires from politics in April 2003.

The 2002 annual military reshuffle provided an opportunity for the prime minister to engineer the appointment of relatives to the head of the armed forces. This resulted in considerable unrest among the top brass of the armed forces, requiring General Prem Tinsulanonda, an elder statesman and a former prime minister, to strongly call for harmony and unity in the ranks in the aftermath of the shuffle.

Relations with the highly independent press have also been controversial throughout the prime minister's tenure. In fact, he had a history of conflict with the media prior to taking office. In 2002, there were instances where visas were withdrawn for foreign correspondents, bans placed on radio and television broadcasts, editors jailed following libel suits, and media companies investigated by the government. The government has also failed so far to establish two independent organizations stipulated by the 1997 Constitution that might have counterbalanced the prime minister's influence: the National Broadcasting Commission and the National Telecommunication Commission. Some members of the media are apparently exercising self-censorship, but on the whole, Thai journalists remain free and willing to criticize abuse in the government.

With the increase of power around the prime minister, there is concern in some quarters about the integrity of the three agencies—the Election Commisssion, the National Counter Corruption Commission, and the Constitutional Courts—established by the 1997 Constitution to safeguard Thai democracy. In the absence of an effective opposition in the National Assembly, these are the agencies Thai citizens rely on to ensure fair elections and control corruption and abuse of power in government. The danger is that Thais are so critical of the political processes that they are tempted to politicize them, either by opposition parties seeking to press charges that they cannot push in the parliament or by the prime minister's party support through amendments to the Constitution or the appointment processes. So far, however, this has not happened and there remains strong public support for the independent agencies.

On the economic side, Thaksin's political position is bolstered by a strong rebound of the Thai economy over the past year. Despite the extensive criticism of his populist policies by professional economists, the government's mix of heavy subsidies and loose monetary policies has boosted consumer spending and business confidence and produced the illusion of growth. Government figures indicate that the growth rate topped 5 percent in the second and third quarters of 2002. Foreign exchange reserves stand at more than US$38 billion, allowing Thailand to repay the last installment of US$1 billion of its Asian economic crisis loan to the International Monetary Fund (IMF) in January 2003, a year ahead of the deadline.

The longer-term health of the economy, however, remains in doubt. The government is spending beyond its means. Bad loans remain stubbornly high. State banks have been ordered to set lending targets, potentially leading to more nonperforming loans.

Since Thailand has relatively open borders and a large tourist economy, the public has been concerned about a growth in transnational criminal behavior and terrorism, and concern became more palpable following the bombings in Bali on October 12, 2002. The government denies reports that the Bali bombings might have been planned in Thailand, and downplays what it regards as exaggerated foreign rhetoric and misleading foreign travel advisories about the dangers to Thai tourists traveling to island destinations in southern Thailand. In reality, however, the Thai security agencies are alarmed about cross-border movements of terrorists and potential terrorism in Thailand itself and have been cooperating closely with their international counterparts in exchanging intelligence and closing bank accounts linked to terrorist groups.

EXTERNAL Thailand's major external security threats come from cross-border illegal activity rather than any direct conventional threat from a foreign government. Of the bordering countries, the relationship with Myanmar (Burma) remains the most contentious and challenging. Thailand has been concerned about ethnic tensions that spill across into Thai territory and the drug smuggling across the long, difficult-to-police border. There is some indication that the Yangon authorities are beginning to crack down on the trade in heroin even while profiting from the large-scale cross-border trafficking in methamphetamines by Wa drug lords. Following the direction of Thaksin, the military has been placed in a coordinating position on these border issues to some dismay among other Thai security-related agencies.

While the drug, ethnic, and cross-border incursions by Myanmarese forces are clearly a legitimate concern for Thailand, Thai involvement in human rights struggles within Myanmar is a matter of some internal debate. Some Thai nongovernmental organizations argue that Thailand should take a strong interest, not just on moral grounds but also because the suppression of human rights is a fundamental cause of the border problems as well as the large-scale flow of refugees and illegal migrants. However, the Thai authorities have overlooked human rights violations in Myanmar in order to promote amicable government-to-government relations.

Thailand also enjoys good relations with Laos and Cambodia. The Laotian and Thai governments are cooperating on building a second border bridge and a road link from Chaing Rai to China via Laos's Bo Kaeo province. However, the Vientiane government continues to be dissatisfied with the lack of Thai action on an extradition request for 28 suspects in an attack on a Laotian customs office in July 2000.

The prime minister also has been active in diplomacy through the Association of Southeast Asian Nations (ASEAN) and, with the rapid turnover of ASEAN leaders, may soon become one of the organization's most senior leaders. The agendas for his trips within the ASEAN group are to forge bilateral cooperation in suppressing terrorism networks and promote economic and trade relations.

Farther afield, the prime minister is active in international affairs, generally traveling abroad on an average of more than once a month. Recent official visits have been to the United States, the United Kingdom, China, Japan, Russia, India, and Australia. Illustrative of his personal interest in diplomacy, Thaksin launched the concept of "CEO ambassadors" in March 2002 using six embassies on a trial basis, and he made it clear at the annual Thai ambassadors' meeting in August 2002 that the ambassadors should directly report to his office.

In relations with the United States, Thai cooperation with anti-terrorism has been praised by U.S. Ambassador Darryl Johnson and Federal Bureau of Investigation (FBI) Director Robert Mueller. Concrete evidence is the first Thai-U.S. anti-terrorist war game in Thailand, code-named Known Warrior and held in August. It involved 1,000 Thai military personnel and about 500 U.S. military officers from the U.S. Pacific Command. The two governments are seeking to strengthen intelligence coordination, installation of a suspected-terrorist entry warning system, and monitoring of terrorist movements with a view toward making Thailand a regional anti-terrorist center.

DEFENSE POLICIES AND ISSUES

DEFENSE BUDGET   The government is allocating about B80 billion (US$1.86 billion at US$1 = B43.03) to defense in a total national budget for 2003 of B999.99 billion (US$23.24 billion). Some of the new procurements are for anti-smuggling and anti-terrorism purposes. Last year's navy request to purchase two submarines was scaled back to a lease, although two British frigates are being purchased on the barter-trade agreement with the British government. Two offshore patrol boats worth B3.52 billion (US$81.8 million) may be purchased from China. To boost the capability of the anti-drug Task Force 399, the Thai government will place 33 more orders for Blackhawk helicopters. In addition, the air force seeks to replace ejector seats of its 40 Alpha Jet fleet. The army has selected the Third Special Warfare Division's combat unit to be its main line of military defense against terrorism. This unit will be equipped with MP-5 electric rifles and other high-technology weapons.

Thailand continues its engagement with a foreign military exercise, which is the annual Thai-U.S. joint military exercise codenamed Cobra Gold. In 2002, some 14,000 U.S. and 7,000 Thai personnel were involved, and 18 other countries participated as observers. As in the previous year's exercise, major components of the exercise were to fight drug trafficking and biochemical terrorists. Thailand is considering a proposal for setting up the Joint Rapid Reaction Command with the British government. The primary purpose is to serve as a bastion for anti-terrorism operations.

CONTRIBUTIONS TO REGIONAL AND GLOBAL SECURITY

Thailand is an active participant in international efforts to fight terrorism and cross-border crimes and contributes to UN peacemaking and peacekeeping. Increasingly, counter-terrorism lies at the core of the government's security planning. Under the prime minister's chairmanship, the National Security Council drafted and adopted a five-year strategic plan to counter transnational crimes, including terrorism. Funding for intelligence agencies is being increased. At the multilateral level, Thailand is a party to various multilateral conventions and protocols aimed at combating terrorism including the Convention on Offenses and Certain Other Acts Committed on Board Aircraft 1963 (Tokyo Convention), the Convention for the Suppression of Unlawful Seizure of

Aircraft 1970 (The Hague Convention), and the Convention for the Suppression of Unlawful Acts against the Safety of Civil Aviation 1971 (Montreal Convention).

The government realizes these conventions focus almost exclusively on threats to aviation. Therefore, the NSC and other related agencies are exploring the possibility of joining other multilateral agreements such as the Convention for the Suppression of Unlawful Acts against the Safety of Maritime Navigation 1988 and the Convention on the Marking of Plastic Explosives for the Purpose of Detection 1991. At the ASEAN Foreign Ministers' Meeting in Phuket, the Thai foreign minister declared that the region is united in fighting terrorism. In addition, Thailand is a party to the joint ASEAN-U.S.agreement on combating terrorism, announced in Brunei in August.

Following the Bali bombings, the Thai government has stepped up efforts to track down the suspected terrorists who may have fled from neighboring Indonesia, Malaysia, or Singapore. The Fourth Army's intelligence units maintain close cooperation with their counterparts in these neighboring countries in order to monitor potential al Qaeda movements. The exact extent of the Jemaah Islamiah (JI) network in Southeast Asia, its relationship with al Qaeda, and its presence in Thailand are all still unknown, but clearly the Thais intend to work closely with their ASEAN neighbors in trying to contain this threat.

An extensive effort has gone into fighting widespread illegal drug trafficking. The Third Army has set up five crack units along the Burmese border to support anti-drug operations, deploying its two new Blackhawk helicopters to ferry task forces for any rapid operation. Thailand is cooperating with China, Laos, and Myanmar to curb the increasing volume of drug trafficking on the Mekong waterway. Thailand has received support in Washington for its proposal to establish an international police headquarters that focuses on drug control. It is likely that the anti-drug Task Force 399 will be upgraded to an operation center reporting directly to the Thai army.

Human trafficking is another concern, especially across Thailand's borders with Myanmar, Cambodia, and Laos. The Thai government was active in organizing a region-wide conference in October to discuss the ways and means to curb these activities.

Terrorism, drug smuggling, and human trafficking use money laundering for making payments and maintaining profits. The Thai government has support from the British government and the European Commission for training personnel to control money laundering. They provide half of the €1.2 million (US$1.25 million at €1 = US$1.04) budget, while the Thai Anti-Money Laundering Office (AMLO) provides additional support.

Other international contributions include the recent ratification of the Kyoto Protocol on greenhouse gases and an offer to host a September 2003 conference on the full implementation of the International Landmine Treaty. Former Foreign Minister Surin Pitsuwan serves on the World Commission on the Social Dimension of Globalization, and former Deputy Prime Minister Supachai Panichpakdi is now the director-general of the World Trade Organization (WTO).

Thailand has been active in peacekeeping activities. By request of the Norwegian government, it serves as the location for discussions between the Sri Lankan government and the Liberation Tigers of Tamil Eelam (LTTE), having served as a venue for three rounds of negotiations in 2002 and early 2003.

Thailand also played a large and multifaceted role in peacekeeping and reconstruction in East Timor. Thai soldiers monitored the general election there, and the Department of Technical and Economic Cooperation (DTEC) carried out rehabilitation projects. The Thai government also is running a village-training development program for village heads in East Timor.

In the case of Afghanistan, Thailand attended the donor countries' conference in Tokyo in January 2002, and proposed an opium substitution plan for Afghanistan. The Thai cabinet is spending B215 million (US$5 million) to deploy 130 army engineers to Afghanistan to assist in the repair of airfields.

Finally, given the plan of the United Nations to make Thailand a regional training center for peacekeeping operations, the organization strongly supports Thailand to host the world's first peacekeeping seminar.

18 United States

THE SECURITY ENVIRONMENT

In the months immediately following the terrorist attacks of September 11, 2001, U.S. foreign and security policy remained tightly focused on the war against al Qaeda and the group's Afghan support base. Southeast Asia also claimed attention in the war on terrorism due to rapidly growing evidence of al Qaeda–affiliated networks in the region. With the Taliban routed and al Qaeda dispersed from Afghanistan, the Bush administration's principal attention shifted toward "regime change" in Iraq. In East Asia, Iraq became an important theme in relations with Japan, China, and the Muslim states of Southeast Asia. But despite impending military action against Baghdad, the White House was forced to devote increased attention to another regional security issue—a rapidly escalating crisis with North Korea over its nuclear weapons program. Meanwhile, concern over terrorist activities, real and potential, remained high on the Southeast Asia agenda.

INTERNAL   Two subjects dominate the U.S. domestic scene: the economy and terrorist concerns. The economy of 2002–2003 presents a striking contrast to that of two or three years earlier. The boom years of the Clinton administration characterized by rapid economic growth of the gross domestic product, stratospheric equity markets, and record budget surpluses seem a distant memory. With sluggish growth, stagnant tax receipts, tax cuts, and rapidly rising defense spending, the federal budget is awash in red ink. Nevertheless, the administration has had little difficulty in generating support for large new defense and

161

anti-terrorism expenditures. To kick-start the economy, the administration is also proposing further tax cuts.

Terrorism and related concerns continue to fray the nerves of citizens —particularly in and around the nation's capital and other major urban centers. Fresh memories of the airliner attacks on the World Trade Center and the Pentagon (and a barely averted companion attack on the Capitol or the White House), the failure to solve the subsequent anthrax bio-terrorism case, periodic warnings and arrests of suspected terrorist "sleeper cells," and random killings in Washington, D.C., by a serial sniper all make homeland security more than a theoretical proposition.

Despite the weak economy and some opposition to his internal security proposals, President George W. Bush remains highly popular in the country at large. The November 2002 midterm congressional elections reinforced his position when his Republican Party defied historical trends to retain its majority position in the House of Representatives and regain a narrow majority in the Senate. The president's popularity and political barnstorming on behalf of his party's candidates were widely regarded as a factor critical to the midterm results. The White House, however, realizes that nothing can be taken for granted in politics and used the period immediately after the election to reshuffle its economic team. Concern that any future attacks would be laid at the door of the administration also helps to drive the strong focus on anti-terrorism.

EXTERNAL   From a U.S. perspective, the East Asia Pacific security environment is characterized by a combination of long-established and newly emergent issues. In the former category is the growing power and prominence of China. China's steady emergence as a regional great power rests on the remarkable sustained growth of the economy, which in turn supports marked increases in defense spending. A sophisticated Chinese diplomatic effort (including a proposal for a free trade area among China and the member states of the Association for Southeast Asian Nations [ASEAN]) focused on Southeast Asia has paid off with growing Chinese influence in that region. The emerging contours of a geopolitical contest between China and the United States in Southeast Asia are evident.

Japan, by contrast, remains mired in a decade-long economic slump reflecting the inability of its political and corporate leadership to confront the burden of bad commercial debt created when the "bubble economy" of the 1980s and early 1990s burst. And while South Korea is generally regarded as having successfully reformed its economy after the 1997 Asian economic crisis, there is growing concern in Washington about increased "anti-American" sentiments in the country—fueled at least in part by the belief that U.S. hard-line policies are largely responsible for the belligerent posture of the North. From the perspective of the Bush administration, Pyongyang is an "evil" regime that devotes most of its resources to its military, holds its own people to cruel, exploitative conditions, provides weapons and weapons technology to dangerous customers, and continues to seek weapons of mass destruction (WMD). North Korea's nuclear program was believed to have been contained by the 1994 Agreed Framework under which an international consortium was building light-water reactors for the North Koreans with heavy fuel oil supplied in the interim, while the North closed its nuclear reactors and kept its spent fuel rods in storage under the supervision and monitoring of the International Atomic Energy Agency (IAEA). But in late 2002, Pyongyang admitted the existence of a clandestine uranium enrichment program for weapons purposes and terminated IAEA monitoring of its plutonium facilities.

Southeast Asia before September 11 was very much on the strategic backburner from Washington's perspective. The principal concerns centered on Indonesia's very difficult political and economic recovery from the Asian financial crisis and the fall of the Suharto regime.

In American eyes, all issues were immediately subordinated to the war on terrorism in the wake of September 11. Japan responded with offers of naval assistance to the U.S. campaign in Afghanistan. China quickly sought to align itself with the U.S. anti-terrorist campaign, citing its own difficulties with Muslim militants in its western interior. Although Southeast Asia is home to a significant portion of the world's Muslims, most analysts did not expect the region to become a major theater in the war on terrorism. This was a miscalculation. Singapore, Malaysia, and the Philippines all announced the arrests of alleged al Qaeda–affiliated operatives after September 11. A major bomb plot targeting the U.S. Embassy in Singapore was thwarted. Prime Minister Mahathir bin Mohammed publicly enlisted Malaysia in the war on terrorism and began a crackdown on hardcore Islamists. Washington and Manila publicly identified the violent splinter group, Abu Sayyaf, as having ties (at least at one time) to al Qaeda. Indonesia was more reluctant in cracking down on or even admitting the existence of domestic militants until the destructive bombings in Bali in October 2002.

The Jakarta authorities then responded by acknowledging the presence of al Qaeda in Indonesia and by instituting tough new anti-terrorist measures.

DEFENSE POLICIES AND ISSUES

NATIONAL SECURITY STRATEGY STATEMENT   The Bush administration issued its formulation of the *National Security Strategy of the United States of America* in September 2002. In many respects, it is a remarkable document—clearly shaped by the experience of September 11 and the anticipation of a probable military campaign against Iraq. The contrast with its 1996 predecessor issued by the Clinton administration is striking. The earlier document evoked the optimism of the post–cold war environment, calling for the "enlargement" of the democratic realm and "engagement" with former adversaries. It assumed the primary importance of economic growth and commerce and provided a rationale for the deployment of U.S. armed forces in diverse and far-flung peacekeeping and humanitarian operations.

The current formulation more clearly moves beyond the cold war era and strikes a very different tone—urgent, assertive, even belligerent—against the backdrop of mortal threat. In essence, the document argues that the United States and other free nations face a new and unprecedented menace at this moment in history from international terrorism and WMD. Faced with this transcendent danger, the United States has no choice but to take whatever actions its security requires, including, if necessary, preemptive attacks against its enemies. From this perspective, the events of September 11 were a critical wake-up call alerting the nation to the gathering peril.

The Bush document paints a world of black and white where the terms "good" and "evil" mean something and where policy must embody values—freedom above all. In the president's words: "Some worry that it is somehow undiplomatic or impolite to speak the language of right and wrong. I disagree. Different circumstances require different methods, but not different moralities." The battle the president invokes is one of survival, but it is also a moral crusade.

The threat is perceived to emerge out of the lethal combination of weak states, ideological radicalism, and WMD technology. The enemy that emerges from this toxic brew is terrorism—specifically terrorist organizations often supported by "rogue states." The defining characteristics of such states—they "brutalize their own people," " display no regard for international law," "sponsor terrorism," "reject basic human values," and are "determined to acquire WMD"—add up to the Bush administration's profile of Iraq.

The weapons in this contest must include "every tool in our arsenal" (military, diplomatic, economic, intelligence, public affairs) and homeland defense. Allies and friends must be enlisted, international institutions must be strengthened, regional conflicts must be defused, and those able and willing to use assistance must be helped. But the centerpiece of this effort will be to "maintain defenses beyond challenge." Lest there be any doubt, the strategy states: "Our forces will be strong enough to dissuade potential adversaries from pursuing a military buildup in hopes of surpassing, or equaling, the power of the United States."

Underlining the importance of allies and "friends," the document lauds the post–September 11 support offered by a number of Asia Pacific nations (along with others), including Australia, Japan, South Korea, Thailand, the Philippines, and New Zealand. ASEAN and the Asia-Pacific Economic Cooperation (APEC) forum are cited as necessary elements in "a mix of regional and bilateral strategies to manage change in this dynamic region." Finally, Australia and Singapore are mentioned as "focal points" in negotiating new bilateral free trade agreements.

ASIAN SECURITY ISSUES   The area of responsibility (AOR) of the U.S. Pacific Command encompasses all of East Asia plus the Pacific islands and most of South Asia. Despite this unified command and overarching security concerns that encompass the entire Asia Pacific, U.S. security planners tend to see the area in terms of two subregions: Northeast Asia (including China and Taiwan) and Southeast Asia. The issues and the policy responses to them tend to be distinctive and specific to each subregion.

The current security picture in Northeast Asia is remarkably dynamic. In macro-terms, a marked shift in the balance of power is under way to the benefit of China and the detriment of Japan. Of the two principal flashpoints in the subregion—Taiwan/China and North Korea —the former has been relatively quiescent whereas the latter rapidly assumed crisis proportions in late 2002 and early 2003.

China's status as an emerging regional great power reflects growing Chinese capabilities (economic and military) given direction and impetus by great power aspirations. In Washington's eyes, much of the irritability in U.S.-China relations can be traced to a conviction among Chinese officials and populace alike that the United States is determined to deny China its birthright as a great power.

In fact, U.S. strategic opinion, both in and outside the government, is divided on China. A body of hawkish analysis sees the growth of Chinese power as inevitably inimical to U.S. interests. The logical inference is that U.S. policy should seek to curtail that growth and prepare for the likelihood of a U.S.-China conflict in the longer term. A far larger, but less cohesive, body of opinion sees a rising China as a work in progress and one susceptible to influence by well-conceived U.S. policies. These policies would be designed to persuade the Chinese leaders over time that their best interests are served by a strategic acceptance of an Asia that accommodates the emergence of a China that is wealthy, influential, and powerful—but not a hegemon. Each of the schools finds support for its interpretation in China's current development and foreign and defense policies.

Since September 11, there has been a notable improvement in the bilateral climate with Beijing seeing an opportunity to repair a badly frayed relationship and Washington seeing a potentially helpful collaborator in the war on terrorism. Beijing pledged its support for the U.S. campaign against the Taliban and has raised no public objections to the sudden presence of American military power in Central Asia. Nor has China registered any concerns over a return of U.S. forces to the Philippines or closer security ties between Washington, Kuala Lumpur, and Singapore. In return, Deputy Secretary of State Richard Armitage visited China and announced that the United States was adding the principal Uighur separatist organization to the U.S. list of terrorist entities. Consequently, U.S. efforts to obtain a UN Security Council resolution supporting the Bush administration position on Iraq ran into heavier resistance in Paris and Moscow than in Beijing.

Some analysts have gone so far as to suggest that counter-terrorism may provide a new strategic framework for U.S.-China relations. But there will be complexities and pitfalls on this road, notably Taiwan. The status of the island remains a painful and potentially explosive issue with U.S. officials increasingly supportive of Taiwan's security and its democratization, while the Chinese government at Beijing remains adamant about reunification.

The triangular relationship between Taiwan, China, and the United States has undergone significant change in the last two years. The Bush administration has moved U.S. policy away from "strategic ambiguity" to an assertion that the United States would do "whatever it took," in the words of President Bush, to help Taiwan defend itself. The White House approved of a substantial list of U.S. weapons for sale to Taiwan, and positive sentiments toward Taiwan have likewise increased in Congress. Along with the rise of the traditional pro-independence Democratic People's Party on Taiwan, there is plenty of potential for a serious crisis, except that currently none of the parties wants one. One reason for this is that an important part of the triangular picture is the rapid growth of interdependent economic ties among all three parties. Economic interests in all three seek political stability in the relationships.

Japan presents a strong contrast to China. Once also thought to be a challenger to U.S. preeminence, its declining economic fortunes have markedly alleviated former trade tensions, while Japan's own apprehensions about China's rise have tended toward a tightening of its political relationship with the United States. The U.S. trade deficit with Japan dropped sharply in 2001 to US$69 billion from US$81 billion the year before. American concerns have shifted toward Japan's chronic problems of bad debt in the banking sector and deflation, producing increasingly pointed urgings from Washington for effective action. Behind these expressions, close observers detect the first signs of a declining U.S. regard for a country that remains an important military ally. Yet, there is at the same time a dawning perception in Washington and Tokyo that the two countries share a fundamental strategic interest in cooperating vis-à-vis China. Whether that interest will produce any tangible security initiatives remains to be seen.

Meanwhile, North Korea has become the most urgent issue on the East Asian security agenda at the beginning of 2003. The Bush administration came into office harboring strong reservations concerning the "Sunshine Policy" of South Korean President Kim Dae Jung toward North Korea as well as the previous policies of the Clinton administration. President Bush publicly grouped Pyongyang with Tehran and Baghdad as an "axis of evil." Nevertheless, the administration downplayed the revelation in October 2002 that Pyongyang had admitted to a uranium enrichment program in violation of the Framework Agreement. A general consensus quickly emerged in official Washington that the North Korean program was probably intended as a bargaining chip to be exchanged for diplomatic and economic concessions—primarily from the United States. The Bush administration refused further discussion with North Korea until it lived up to its commitments and in December cut off heavy oil supplies. The North Koreans reacted by disabling IAEA monitoring equipment, ejecting the international monitors, and loading fuel into one of the reactors, thus suddenly presenting a much more dangerous proliferation threat than was coming from the embryonic uranium enrichment program. Washington is seeking support from Tokyo, Seoul, Beijing, and Moscow for putting a coordinated strategy of pressure on North Korea, exploiting that country's extreme economic vulnerability, to force it to reverse course. North Korea is not playing this game, and the other countries essential to such a strategy are not signed on board. South Korea is a critical player, and the victory of Kim Dae Jung protégé Roh Moo Hyun in the December presidential election makes it likely that Seoul's Sunshine Policy will continue. The challenge for Washington is to contain the proliferation threat while not endangering its Asian alliances or diverting attention from what it regards as the more immediate Iraq problem.

U.S. strategy toward Southeast Asia since the end of the Vietnam War in 1975 had lacked a sharp focus and clear priorities. There was no tangible, credible threat, but this changed after September 11, particularly when Washington determined that al Qaeda had established at least a toehold in Muslim Southeast Asia through a relationship with the Indonesia-based Jemaah Islamiah (JI)—sufficient for the president to declare the region a "second front" in America's global war on terrorism. Within the region, U.S. counter-terrorism concerns focused sharply on the Philippines, Singapore, Malaysia, and Indonesia. In the Philippines, U.S. assistance has taken the form of Special Forces assisting Philippine army units hunting Abu Sayyaf guerrillas, who were holding two U.S. hostages, and larger joint exercises between the United States and the Philippines armed forces on Luzon. President Gloria Macapagal Arroyo has made it clear that she sees these activities as steps in reestablishing robust and sustained military-to-military cooperation for the first time since U.S. forces left Subic Bay in 1991.

In Malaysia, Prime Minister Mahathir surprised many after September 11 by quickly staking out a position of common cause with the United States in the global struggle against terrorism. This response is valued and appreciated in Washington as coming from the leader of a predominantly Muslim country. Meanwhile, already close relations with Singapore have become even more seamless in response to the terrorist threat. In both Singapore and Malaysia, the United States has sought and received close security cooperation in the areas of intelligence, police, and customs.

Indonesia has been the primary focus of U.S. anti-terrorism concerns in Southeast Asia since the discovery of the JI network and cells directed and inspired by militant Islamists in Java. For the United States, a major policy conundrum involves the Indonesian National Military (TNI, or Tentara Nasional Indonesia). Under-funded, under-equipped, poorly trained, and politically discredited—the TNI is a wounded institution. And because of its culpability in the East Timor bloodletting, the U.S. Congress imposed a ban on most forms of U.S.-Indonesian military-to-military cooperation. But the Bush administration sees a revitalized TNI as a vital element in a successful counter-terror strategy in Indonesia and more broadly in Southeast Asia. The policy problem facing the Pentagon is how to reestablish an effective assistance program to the TNI while reaffirming congressionally mandated support for military reform and accountability.

Overall, the post–September 11 period is witnessing the first serious refocus of U.S. security priorities toward Southeast Asia since the Vietnam War. But the future effectiveness of American policy will be largely determined by developments within the region. There are many imponderables. Can Manila reach a durable political accommodation with moderate Islamic elements and isolate the militants in the south? Will the Megawati government along with the TNI mount a determined and sustained campaign to control Muslim extremists in Indonesia? Can the leadership of the dominant Malay political party in Malaysia reverse the secular decline in its appeal to the Malay rural population and foreclose the rise of a militant Muslim movement?

In Northeast Asia, the questions involving U.S. policy are more sharply focused. Since the military option is too dangerous, can Washington fashion an effective policy of coercive diplomacy to induce North Korea to once and for all get out of the nuclear weapons business? Can the United States develop and implement a joint security strategy with Japan with regard to China? Can the United States and China reach a strategic understanding that provides room for China's emergence as a regional great power? Can the Taiwan issue continue to be managed?

BUDGET   Donald Rumsfeld assumed the office of secretary of defense committed to an agenda of "defense transformation." Much of that agenda has received a major boost from the experience of September 11 and the subsequent campaign in Afghanistan. Some of the principal aspects of transformation include ever increasing emphasis on electronic warfare—battlefield information systems, networks, sensors, command and control, and all-weather intelligence and surveillance. Another enduring theme is "jointness" and interoperability—the necessity for the various services and components to work together seamlessly. A third element is mobility—forces that are lighter, faster, more lethal, and more deployable. A fourth theme is a "capabilities-based" approach to strategy rather than a threat-based approach. This rests on the proposition that threats have become too protean and unpredictable to be the basis for major procurement decisions. A fifth element arises directly from September 11—homeland security including creation of a new regional command for North America. Ballistic missile defense is a final element that had a very high priority before September 11 and continues to be pushed, but is less clearly reinforced by those events.

In the early months of the administration, Rumsfeld's program conflicted with preexisting priorities in what was perceived as a tight budget environment. The war on terror has had a major impact on congressional receptivity to a rapidly growing defense budget that can accommodate both new and traditional programs. Rumsfeld and the joint chiefs have enjoyed a political environment where resistance to increased defense spending has virtually evaporated. As a result, there have been large increases in the defense budget, to US$331 billion in fiscal year 2002 and US$355 billion in fiscal 2003. The latter does not include massive supplemental budget requests (more than US$40 billion for the army alone). The fiscal 2002 number was US$100 billion greater than just three or four years ago. However, many of the new "transformational" programs are just starting to have a significant budget impact. By fiscal 2004, some tough programmatic choices, so far avoided, will require attention.

Contributions to Regional and Global Security

In U.S. eyes, the American contribution to security in Asia Pacific has been a fundamental prerequisite for the economic transformation of this region since World War II. In strategic terms, U.S. forces have performed three interconnected missions, which all contribute to the unprecedented stability of the region. First, U.S. forces in Korea act as a deterrent against a possible North Korean attack on the South and by extension as a de facto deterrent against a Chinese assault on Taiwan.

Second, forces deployed to and through Southeast Asia act as a kind of security guarantor preventing many not so hidden rivalries and disputes within the region from spiraling out of control. Third, the entire Asia Pacific presence acts as a counterweight (and barrier) to possibly overweening Chinese strategic ambition—for example in the South China Sea. All of these contributions add up to another: preserving international commercial access to the region as a whole. Now another mission has been added to this list—counter-terrorism, particularly in Southeast Asia.

The forces deployed for these purposes belong to the U.S. Pacific Command (PACOM) headquartered in Hawaii. Total personnel under PACOM add up to about 340,000, one-third of which are forward deployed in the region. The latter includes the 7th Fleet (Japan), a Marine Expeditionary Force (Japan/Okinawa), the 5th Air Force (Japan), the 7th Air Force (Korea), and the 8th Army (Korea). The size and distribution of these forces have remained basically stable for the last decade and no major changes are slated for the near future.

Since the departure of U.S. forces from the Philippines, the Pacific Command has had the problem of maintaining a credible presence in Southeast Asia. This requirement has been met through frequent naval and air deployments utilizing bilaterally negotiated access agreements with many of the ASEAN countries. The lynchpin of this regional presence is Singapore, which is host to a small permanent PACOM headquarters element as well as regular air and naval deployments. Unique in the region, Singapore has constructed a pier complex to accommodate U.S. aircraft carriers.

Diplomatically, the United States is heavily engaged bilaterally and multilaterally in the region. While a relatively small group of countries are formal allies, including Japan, South Korea, the Philippines, Thailand, and Australia, many others have close security and political ties with the United States. Multilateral diplomacy is focused on the ASEAN Regional Forum (ARF), the ASEAN Post-Ministerial Meeting, and APEC forum. While American officials frequently express frustration with the difficulties of moving forward practical forms of cooperation in these multilateral forums, senior officials regularly attend and make good use of the opportunity to meet counterparts in side-meetings. They have been highly appreciative of the support these organizations have given to the anti-terrorism effort, helping to build the international norms and cooperation mechanisms needed for effective action in this area.

Aside from the contribution the U.S. security and diplomatic presence makes to the region's order and prosperity, the U.S. economy is critical to growth in most of the Asia Pacific economies. Although its bilateral foreign assistance programs are small, the United States is a major provider of investment capital and technology throughout the region, and by far the region's largest market for manufactured goods.

19 Vietnam

THE SECURITY ENVIRONMENT

INTERNAL   Vietnam is continuing the process of renewal by further accelerating political and economic reforms. In the political sphere, 99.7 percent of Vietnamese voters went to the polls in May 2002 to elect 498 candidates to the 11th National Assembly. In July, the new National Assembly approved the cabinet at its first session, indicating a strong commitment to renewal. Responding to criticism of sluggishness in moving ahead with administrative reforms, the new government's priorities include reenforcing supervision, tightening administrative discipline, and clearly fixing accountability and defining the relationship between government bodies. The government also is focusing on fighting corruption and waste, red tape, smuggling, and, in particular, the abuse of positions of power to achieve illegal wealth. Finally, in a move toward building a more democratic and transparent administrative apparatus, the government adopted new legislative procedures requiring public input and approval on all laws, ordinances, and administrative decrees concerning the socioeconomic well-being of large sections of the population. These administrative reforms are being implemented at all echelons.

In the economic field, the new government is strengthening the equity program of state-owned enterprises (SOEs) by promising more autonomy to local authorities and adopting more liberal policies and simplified procedures. The pace of the overall SOE reform has slowed down and a number of issues lie at the heart of this problem. As of late May 2002, only 800 SOEs had been equitized in a decade of reform, accounting for just 15 percent of SOEs or just 2.5 percent of the total state sector. The government is implementing a plan to reduce the present 5,600 SOEs to 2,000 by 2005 and to decentralize further decision-making. Foreigners are entitled to buy up to 30 percent of the shares in equitized businesses under the 80 percent export requirement provisions.

Economic growth is regarded as a key to national security. Vietnam is currently one of East Asia's fastest growing economies, with gross domestic product growth of 7.04 percent during 2002. To nudge the economy up further, the government is stopping preferential credits from state funds to many kinds of less productive projects and leveling the playing ground for domestic as well as foreign investors. It has pledged to remove administrative barriers at the grass-roots level. Export growth rate was only 10 percent in 2002, falling short of the target. Aside from the weakened state of the world economy, internal barriers boost the production and service costs of a number of Vietnamese products, reducing the international competitiveness. Shortcomings in investment and construction also led to low investment efficiency.

Tourism is a bright spot in the Vietnamese economy. The country's image as a safe, stable, and friendly destination helped attract a record number of 2.6 million tourists, an increase of 14 percent over last year, with total revenue of US$1.53 billion. Along with improved tourism, Vietnam Airlines is poised to become a major carrier in Southeast Asia. During 2002, it carried four million passengers (2.24 million domestic travelers and 1.76 million foreigners).

Remittances are another source of income. Nearly 43,000 Vietnamese workers and experts were sent to 40 countries and territories in 2002, bringing the total number of Vietnamese nationals working abroad to more than 310,000.

. Foreign investment is a driving force in Vietnam's economy. The foreign direct investment (FDI) sector grossed a turnover of US$9 billion in 2002, which, excluding revenue from oil and gas industries, was an increase of 10 percent. Disbursed capital for foreign investments reached US$2.34 billion, marking an 11 percent year-on-year increase. The year also saw an additional 100 foreign-invested projects that went into operation. Vietnam now hosts more than 1,800 projects with a total prescribed capital of US$25 billion. The FDI sector now accounts for 25 percent of the country's total industrial value and 27 percent of its exports, not counting oil and gas. Another 700 new FDI projects were licensed in 2002 with a total prescribed capital of US$1.4 billion. However, FDI directly provided only 0.3 percent of overall employment. Under the new policies, FDI would be expected to contribute 15 percent to GDP and 25 percent to the export turnover during 2001–2005. In 2003, the Vietnamese government is expected to take bold measures, such as further opening to foreign investors hitherto prohibited sectors like real estate and services, facilitating foreign access to equitized firms, reducing electricity and telecommunications charges, eliminating the dual price system for local and foreign companies, and simplifying foreign investment procedures.

Vietnam has begun an ambitious program to reduce the number of poverty-level households from last year's 16 percent to less than 10 percent by 2010. Despite many economic difficulties, the government is pledged to carry out the Poverty Reduction and Hunger Eradication Program by providing a generous fund for the task. The United Nations Development Programme (UNDP) Human Development Report 2002 shows that Vietnam's Human Development Index (HDI) has climbed from 0.682 in 2001 to 0.688 in 2002. Vietnam ranks 43 out of 89 countries in terms of HDI in the UNDP report, an improvement of two places compared to last year's ranking. In addition, about 600,000 new jobs have been created, and the number of households under the poverty line has fallen to 15 percent.

Over the past few years, smuggling and commercial fraud have impeded Vietnam's development. Many anti-smuggling and commercial fraud forces have been set up at both ministerial and local levels, including the Border Guard Force. Vietnam is also clamping down on drugs after discovering that the illicit trade and trafficking of synthetic drugs has increased dramatically over the past year. Aside from crime, embezzlement, wastefulness, and tax dodging, modernization has brought a series of new law and order issues including ecological destruction and a major increase in traffic accidents in urban centers.

Another internal security problem that arose in early 2002 was the illegal border crossing of minority people from the western highlands into Cambodia. The Vietnamese government believes that efforts to destabilize the country by external forces were behind this movement. Vietnam is effectively cooperating with the United Nations High Commissioner on Refugees (UNHCR) and Cambodia to execute the January 2002 tripartite agreement on the repatriation of Vietnamese ethnic-minority citizens who illegally immigrated to Cambodia.

EXTERNAL Vietnam currently enjoys good relations with all other countries. With its most immediate neighbors, border issues and trade dominate the relationships. Vietnam and China are continuing to make good progress on demarcating their 839-mile land border. The ongoing placement of markers will be completed by 2005, the time frame agreed upon after the signing of the Land Border Treaty in December 1999. The completion of markers will be followed by a protocol on border delineation and marker placement, as well as a new treaty on border regulations.

In economic relations, Sino-Vietnamese trade reached US$2.8 billion in 2001 and is expected to increase to US$3.5 billion in 2002 and US$5 billion by 2005. China supports Vietnam's accession to the World Trade Organization (WTO) and waives bilateral negotiations to smooth the way. It has also pledged to upgrade the Thai Nguyen Steel Mill and the Ha Bac Fertilizer Plant, both of which were built with help from the Chinese government. China currently has 114 investment projects in Vietnam with a total capital of US$214 million, ranking 20th among the 65 investor countries in Vietnam.

Vietnam and Laos in 2002 celebrated the 40th anniversary of the establishment of diplomatic relations and the silver jubilee anniversary of their Treaty of Friendship and Cooperation. The treaty continues to provide a firm legal basis for expanding and strengthening the special ties between the two countries. These ties are a priority for both countries and a key factor in the reform process in each. They are improving bilateral cooperation on a variety of security issues, including such human security issues as the fight against crime, cross-border smuggling, and drug trafficking. The two countries are boosting trade and economic cooperation and focusing on social and economic development along their border. They also signed a new agreement in Vientiane in August 2002 to create favorable trading conditions for their businesses. Both governments give priority to the installation of border markers in order to build friendship and facilitate trade. Vietnam continues to train Lao officials and provide agricultural assistance programs.

Modern Vietnamese-Cambodian relations are in their 36th year since the establishment of diplomatic relations. Despite problems in the past, the current relationship is excellent and continues to develop through exchanges, trade, and practical measures that combat issues of common concern. Again, border issues play a critical role. The two countries established a Joint Border Commission, which will be continuing its efforts to develop full understanding on all related issues. Meanwhile, the two countries have agreed to open or expand seven border gates. Vietnam and Cambodia have, together with Laos, pledged to take drastic measures to combat drug trafficking by exchanging information and cooperating in patrolling their common borders. The military dimension of growing Cambodian-Vietnamese cooperation was symbolized by the recent visit to Vietnam of the commander of the Cambodian Royal Navy, General Ung Somkhan.

Political ties between Vietnam and Japan were reinforced by the October 2002 visit to Japan by Communist Party General Secretary Nong Duc Manh and the April 2002 visit to Vietnam by Prime Minister Koizumi Jun'ichirō. Vietnam and Japan have vowed to "act together and advance together" and promote their friendly, cooperative relationship in the spirit of "long-term stability and mutual trust" built upon equal partnership. Japan believes that its broad cooperation with Vietnam could become the engine driving Japan's relations with the Association of Southeast Asian Nations (ASEAN). The two countries believe that an early signing of the Japan-Vietnam Agreement for Investment Liberalization, Promotion and Protection would invigorate economic activities in the region and contribute to the success of the Initiative for Japan-ASEAN Comprehensive Economic Partnership proposed by Prime Minister Koizumi in January 2002. Vietnam supports and welcomes the Japanese Initiative for Development in East Asia (IDEA), and the establishment of a forum for East Asian development at the East Asia Ministerial Meeting held in Tokyo in August. Japanese Official Development Assistance (ODA) has played an important role in Vietnam's national renovation, and at the start of 2002 amounted to US$7.5 billion, making up 40 percent of ODA funds pledged by all donors, a share that is expected to continue to grow. More significantly, the Japanese government has not scaled down the assistance even in the face of its own economic woes. Japan is also Vietnam's largest trade partner, with two-way figures topping US$5 billion in 2001. Japan also accounts for a tenth of all FDI in Vietnam, worth US$3.8 billion.

Vietnam and the United States have agreed on the need to develop a framework for their long-term cooperation that reflects their mutual interests. U.S. Deputy Assistant Secretary of Defense Jerry Jennings visited Vietnam in early August to seek Vietnam's continued support in accounting for U.S. service personnel missing in action during the Vietnam War. The two countries have also agreed to continue to exchange views and bolster cooperation in the fight against crime, especially organized transnational crime, drug trafficking, international terrorism, and money laundering. Since the bilateral trade agreement went into effect last December, bilateral relations have deepened and expanded to new fields. The two-way trade has grown beyond expectations, reaching the US$2 billion mark, with a significant expansion in Vietnam's exports of textiles and garments, and there are now some 800 American companies operating in Vietnam. The U.S. administration has agreed to waive the outdated Jackson-Vanik amendment, which is required for maintaining Normal Trade Relations (NTR) with Vietnam. An important trade issue arises from the charges made by the American Catfish Farmers' Association that 53 Vietnamese catfish processors and exporters are dumping catfish on the U.S. market. The Vietnamese government rejects these allegations and argues that the businesses are operating independently, without subsidies, and making their own free, legal decisions on trade, market, labor hiring, and production costs.

DEFENSE POLICIES AND ISSUES

Vietnam's defense preparations are no longer based on a possible large-scale conventional war of aggression across its borders, but rather on a more complex, multifaceted war of sabotage. To cope with the new concept of threat, its defense forces are being restructured and strengthened in various key places at sea, on islands, at larger border crossings, and in political and economic centers. Defense zones are built at provincial and municipal levels, thus developing a strong defense and security posture and preparing for a people's war posture throughout the country in both peace and wartime. Also in line with the new posture, Vietnam continues to rapidly reduce its regular forces and to strengthen reserve and militia capabilities, thus creating a new balance of the three kinds of forces.

Regarding the Cam Ranh military base issue, all formalities for terminating the May 1979 treaty with the former Soviet Union were completed in July 1, 2002. Vietnam has stated that henceforth the base will be used for Vietnam's national development and defense, and not as a military base in cooperation with any foreign country. This laid to rest lingering anxieties in the region that use of the base might be transferred to another foreign country.

CONTRIBUTIONS TO REGIONAL AND GLOBAL ORDER

Despite its status as a developing country, Vietnam plays an active role in regional and international affairs as a member of ASEAN, the

Asia-Europe Meeting (ASEM), the ASEAN + 3 (China, Japan, and South Korea) process, the Asia-Pacific Economic Cooperation (APEC) forum, and the United Nations. With respect to ASEAN, Vietnam actively contributed to enhancing stronger unity and a narrower development gap among ASEAN members by establishing firm trust among Southeast Asian nations at the 35th ASEAN Ministerial Meeting (AMM), the ASEAN + 3 meeting, and the 9th ASEAN Regional Forum (ARF) meeting. Vietnam was the chair of the ASEAN Inter-Parliamentary Organization (AIPO) during the 2001–2002 term and successfully hosted the 23rd AIPO meeting in September. Vietnam regarded the AIPO General Assembly as an important opportunity for Vietnam to raise its profile in the international community, to boost multifaceted cooperation within the region, and to execute pledges outlined in the ASEAN Hanoi Plan of Action and Hanoi Declaration in July 2001. Vietnam also hosted successfully the first conference of the Fact-Finding Committee to Combat Drug Menace of the AIPO. It also participated in the International Conference on Reconstruction Assistance to Afghanistan held in Tokyo and provided humanitarian aid worth US$300,000 to this country.

Vietnam currently plays a leading role in ASEM as one of the ASEAN coordinators for ASEM and the host of the next summit, ASEM 5, in 2004. Vietnam supports the idea of forming a task force to promote cooperation on trade, economics, and finance between ASEM nations. Vietnam will work closely with other coordinators to inaugurate the task force as soon as possible.

Vietnam was elected to provide one of the vice-presidents of the 57th session of the UN General Assembly held in September and continues to carry out the role until the end of the next session in September 2003. Its election to this important position indicates that Vietnam is highly appreciated by the United Nations and its members, and its international role and prestige are increasing. This, and the country's membership on the UN Human Rights Committee, the UNESCO Executive Council, UNDP, UN Population Fund (UNFPA), and the World Health Organization (WHO), will help it contest a seat as a nonpermanent member of the Security Council in the 2008–2009 term. Vietnam also participated in the UN Special Session on Children and the World Summits on Food Security and on Sustainable Development.

Regarding the fight against terrorism, Vietnam supports all anti-terrorism efforts by the international community on the basis of the UN Charter and international law. It refuses to accept any attempt to use force in the name of combating terrorism, interference in others' internal affairs, or violation of state sovereignty. Vietnam continues to cooperate with the international community to take concerted action to weed out terrorism, but those moves should be carried out in accordance with the UN Charter, international law, and respect for national independence and sovereignty. Vietnam has joined other members of ASEAN, ASEM, APEC, and the United Nations in specific actions against terrorism. It has also called on the United States and other states to join its struggle against anti-Vietnam terrorist plots and moves. Vietnam strongly protests any military acts aimed at toppling an independent and sovereign state and considers military intervention from outside to oust a country's political regime a blatant violation of international law and the UN Charter.

Another area of Vietnamese concern and activism is in the area of illegal immigration and human trafficking, particularly the smuggling of women and children, which has become an important regional and global problem. Poverty, hunger, unemployment, the widening gap between the rich and the poor, environmental problems, natural disasters, and ethnic conflicts are the root causes of illegal immigration.

List of Abbreviations

ABAC APEC Business Advisory Council
ABM Anti-Ballistic Missile (Treaty)
ACP African, Caribbean, and Pacific Group of States
AFP Armed Forces of the Philippines
AIPO ASEAN Inter-Parliamentary Organization
AMLO Anti-Money Laundering Office (Thailand)
AMM ASEAN Ministerial Meeting
AOR area of responsibility
APEC Asia-Pacific Economic Cooperation
ARF ASEAN Regional Forum
ASDF Air Self-Defense Force (Japan)
ASEAN Association of Southeast Asian Nations
ASEAN-ISIS ASEAN Institutes for International and Strategic Studies
ASEM Asia-Europe Meeting
ASG Abu Sayyaf Group (Phillipines)
ASIO Australian Security Intelligence Organization
ASIS Australian Secret Intelligence Service
ASMD Anti-Ship Missile Defense
AVS all-volunteer force (Russia)
AWACS Airborne Warning and Control System
BIMP-EAGA Brunei-Indonesia-Malaysia-Philippines East ASEAN Growth Area
BIMST-EC Bangladesh-India-Myanmar-Sri Lanka-Thailand Economic Cooperation
BJP Bharatiya Janata Party (Indian People's Party)
BRA Bougainville Revolutionary Army (PNG)
CCP Chinese Communist Party
CCS Command and Control System
CHOGM Commonwealth Heads of Government Meetings
CIA Central Intelligency Agency (United States)
CICA Conference on Interaction and Confidence-Building Measures in Asia

CIDA   Canadian International Development Agency
CIS   Commonwealth of Independent States (Russia)
CMC   Central Military Commission (China)
COMELEC   Commisssion on Elections (Philippines)
CPP   Chart Pattana Party (Thailand)
CPP   Communist Party of the Philippines
CSCAP   Council for Security Cooperation in Asia Pacific
CTBT   Comprehensive Test Ban Treaty
DPR   Dewan Perwakilan Rakyat (national parliament, Indonesia)
DSTA   Defense Science and Technology Agency (Singapore)
DTEC   Department of Technical and Economic Cooperation (Thailand)
ECOSOC   UN Economic and Social Council
EEZ   Exclusive Economic Zone
ERC   Economic Review Committee (Singapore)
ERRF   European Rapid Reaction Force
EU   European Union
EW   electronic warfare
EWSP   Electronic Warfare Self Protection
FBI   Federal Bureau of Investigation (United States)
FDI   foreign direct investment
FPDA   Five Power Defense Arrangements (Australia, Malaysia, New Zealand, Singapore, and the United Kingdom)
GAM   Gerakan Aceh Merdeka (Free Aceh Movement, of Indonesia)
GSDF   Ground Self-Defense Force (Japan)
HDI   Human Development Index
IAEA   International Atomic Energy Agency
ICJ   International Court of Justice
IDEA   Initiative for Development in East Asia
IISS   International Institute of Strategic Studies
IMF   International Monetary Fund
INTERFET   International Force in East Timor
IOR-ARC   Indian Ocean Rim Association for Regional Cooperation
ISA   Internal Security Act (Malaysia)
ISAF   International Security Assistance Force
IT   information technology
JCTC   Joint Counter-Terrorism Centre (Singapore)
JI   Jemaah Islamiah
JTF   Joint Task Force

JSC   Joint Staff Council (Japan)
KEDO   Korean Peninsula Energy Development Organization
KMM   Kumpulan Militan Malaysia
LAC   Line of Actual Control (India-China)
LC   Line of Control (India-Pakistan)
LDP   Liberal Democratic Party (Japan)
LTO   Land Transportation Office (Philippines)
LTTE   Liberation Tigers of Tamil Ealam
MAF   Malaysian Armed Forces
MANPADS   Man-Portable Air Defense Systems
MCDV   Maritime Coastal Defense Vessels
MIB   Melayu-Islam-Beraja (Malay-Islamic-Monarchy)
MILF   Moro Islamic Liberation Front (Philippines)
MINDEF   Ministry of Defense (Singapore)
MLRS   multiple launch rocket systems
MLSA   Mutual Logistics Support Agreement (Philippines–United States)
MP   Member of Parliament
MPR   Majelis Permusyawaratan Rakyat (People's Consultative Assembly, of Indonesia)
MPRP   Mongolian People's Revolutionary Party
MSDF   Maritime Self-Defense Force (Japan)
MTDP   Mid-Term Defense Program (Japan)
NAP   New Aspiration Party (Thailand)
NATO   North Atlantic Treaty Organization
NBCD   Nuclear, Biology, and Chemical Defense unit (Malaysia)
NGO   nongovernmental organization
NPA   New People's Army (Philippines)
NPL   nonperforming loans (Japan)
NPT   Nonproliferation Treaty
NSS   National Security Secretariat (Singapore)
NTR   Normal Trade Relations (United States)
OAS   Organization of American States
ODA   Official Development Assistance
OECD   Organization for Economic Co-operation and Development
OIC   Organization of the Islamic Conference
OPM   Organisasi Papua Merdeka (Free Papua Movement)
PACOM   U.S. Pacific Command
PAP   People's Action Party (Singapore)
PAS   Parti Islam SeMalaysia (Islamic Party of Malaysia)

PDI-P   Indonesian Democratic Party-Struggle
PEA   Public Estates Authority (Philippines)
PECC   Pacific Economic Cooperation Council
PLA   People's Liberation Army (China)
PNG   Papua New Guinea
PNGDF   Papua New Guinea Defense Force
PRC   People's Republic of China
RCCSCS   Regional Code of Conduct in the South China Sea
RMAF   Royal Malaysian Air Force
RMN   Royal Malaysian Navy
RSAF   Republic of Singapore Air Force
SAARC   South Asian Association for Regional Cooperation
SACO   Special Action Committee on Okinawa (Japan–United States)
SAF   Singapore Armed Forces
SAFTA   South Asian Free Trade Area
SAS   Special Air Service
SCO   Shanghai Cooperation Organization
SDF   Self-Defense Forces (Japan)
SIS   Security Intelligence Service (New Zealnad)
SOE   state-owned-enterprise
SOFA   Status of Forces Agreement
SPRC   Security Policy Review Committee (Singapore)
TNI   Tentara Nasional Indonesia (Indonesian National Military)
TRT   Thai Rak Thai Party
UAV   Unmanned Aerial Vehicle
UMNO   United Malays National Organization
UN   United Nations
UNCTAD   UN Conference on Trade and Development
UNDP   UN Development Programme
UNESCO   United Nations Educational, Scientific, and Cultural Or-
   gainzation
UNFPA   UN Population Fund
UNHCR   UN High Commissioner for Refugees
UNIFIL   UN Interim Force in Lebanon
UNMEE   UN Mission in Ethiopia and Eritrea
UNMISET   UN Mission of Support in East Timor
UNMOGIP   UN Military Observer Group in India and Pakistan
UNOMIG   UN Observer Mission in Georgia
UNPKO   UN Peacekeeping Operations

UNTAET   UN Transitional Administration in East Timor
UNTSO   UN Truce Supervisory Organization (in Jerusalem)
WHO   World Health Organization
WMD   weapons of mass destruction
WTO   World Trade Organization

The APSO Project Team

A distinctive feature of the *Asia Pacific Security Outlook* is that it is based on background papers developed by analysts from the region. These analysts, many of them younger specialists, meet at an annual workshop to examine each country paper and discuss the overall regional outlook. They also complete a questionnaire on regional security issues, which is used to develop the regional overview and provide an assessment of changing perceptions over time.

Those involved in the process of developing *Asia Pacific Security Outlook 2003* include the following people. (Note: Paper writers participated in their individual capacities; their views do not necessarily represent those of the institutions with which they are affiliated.)

COUNTRY ANALYSTS
(BACKGROUND PAPER WRITER IDENTIFIED BY AN ASTERISK)

AUSTRALIA   Ross Cottrill, Australian Institute of International Affairs*

BRUNEI DARUSSALAM   Pushpathavi Thambipillai, University of Brunei Darussalam*

CANADA   Allen G. Sens and Brian L. Job, University of British Columbia*

CHINA   Chu Shulong, Tsinghua University, Beijing*

EUROPEAN UNION   Sebastian Harnisch, University of Trier, Germany*

INDIA   Dipankar Banerjee, United States Institute of Peace, Washington, D.C.*

INDONESIA   Edy Prasetyono, Centre for Strategic and International Studies, Jakarta*

JAPAN   Katahara Eiichi, Kobe Gakuin University*

REPUBLIC OF KOREA   Chung Oknim, Korean Broadcasting System (KBS), Commentator*

MALAYSIA   Elina Noor, Institute of Strategic and International Studies (ISIS), Kuala Lumpur*

MONGOLIA   Sereeter Galsanjamts, Institute for Strategic Studies, Ulaanbaatar*

NEW ZEALAND David Dickens, New Zealand correspondent to the *Asia-Pacific Defence Reporter**
PAPUA NEW GUINEA Ronald J. May, Australian National University*;
Lt. Col. James Laki, Papua New Guinea National Research Institute
PHILIPPINES Rowena Layador, Institute for Strategic and Development Studies, Quezon City*
RUSSIA Dmitri V. Trenin, Carnegie Moscow Center, Carnegie Endowment for International Peace*
SINGAPORE Irene Ng, Singapore Institute of International Affairs*
THAILAND Chookiat Panaspornprasit, Chulalongkorn University, Bangkok*
UNITED STATES Marvin Ott, National War College, National Defense University, Washington, D.C.*
VIETNAM Ha Hong Hai, Institute for International Relations, Hanoi*

OVERVIEW AND EDITOR

Charles E. Morrison, President, East-West Center

PROJECT DIRECTORS

Charles E. Morrison, President, East-West Center, United States
Jusuf Wanandi, Member of Director Board, Center for Strategic and International Studies, Indonesia
Yamamoto Tadashi, President, Japan Center for International Exchange, Japan

WORKSHOP CO-SPONSORS

Dato' Jawhar bin Hassan, Director-General, Institute of Strategic and International Studies (ISIS), Malaysia
Stephen Leong, Assistant Director-General, Institute of Strategic and International Studies (ISIS), Malaysia

PROJECT COORDINATOR

Wada Shūichi, Japan Center for International Exchange

Index

Asia Pacific Agenda Project

The Asia Pacific Agenda Project (APAP) was established in November 1995 to enhance policy-oriented intellectual exchange at the nongovernmental level, with special emphasis on independent research institutions in the region. It consists of four interconnected components: (1) the Asia Pacific Agenda Forum, a gathering of leaders of Asia Pacific policy research institutes to explore the future agenda for collaborative research and dialogue activities related to the development of an Asia Pacific community; (2) an Asia Pacific policy research information network utilizing the Internet; (3) annual multilateral joint research projects on pertinent issues of regional and global importance undertaken in collaboration with major research institutions in the region; and (4) collaborative research activities designed to nurture a new generation of Asia Pacific leaders who can participate in international intellectual dialogues. APAP is managed by an international steering committee composed of nine major research institutions in the region. The Japan Center for International Exchange has served as secretariat since APAP's inception.

ASEAN Institutes for Strategic and International Studies

ASEAN-ISIS (Institutes for Strategic and International Studies) is an association of nongovernmental organizations registered with the Association of Southeast Asian Nations. Formed in 1988, its membership comprises the Centre for Strategic and International Studies (CSIS) of Indonesia, the Institute of Strategic and International Studies (ISIS) of Malaysia, the Institute for Strategic and Development Studies (ISDS) of the Philippines, the Singapore Institute of International Affairs (SIIA), and the Institute of Security and International Studies (ISIS) of Thailand. Its purpose is to encourage cooperation and coordination of activities among policy-oriented ASEAN scholars and analysts, and to promote policy-oriented studies of, and exchange of information and viewpoints on, various strategic and international issues affecting Southeast Asia's and ASEAN's peace, security, and well-being.

East-West Center

Established by the United States Congress in 1960 to promote mutual understanding and cooperation among the governments and peoples of the Asia Pacific region, including the United States, the East-West Center seeks to foster the development of an Asia Pacific community through cooperative study, training, and research. Center activities focus on the promotion of shared regional values and the building of regional institutions and arrangements; the promotion of economic growth with equity, stability, and sustainability; and the management and resolution of critical regional as well as common problems.

Japan Center for International Exchange

Founded in 1970, the Japan Center for International Exchange (JCIE) is an independent, nonprofit, and nonpartisan organization dedicated to strengthening Japan's role in international affairs. JCIE believes that Japan faces a major challenge in augmenting its positive contributions to the international community, in keeping with its position as one of the world's largest industrial democracies. Operating in a country where policy making has traditionally been dominated by the government bureaucracy, JCIE has played an important role in broadening debate on Japan's international responsibilities by conducting international and cross-sectional programs of exchange, research, and discussion.

JCIE creates opportunities for informed policy discussions; it does not take policy positions. JCIE programs are carried out with the collaboration and cosponsorship of many organizations. The contacts developed through these working relationships are crucial to JCIE's efforts to increase the number of Japanese from the private sector engaged in meaningful policy research and dialogue with overseas counterparts. JCIE receives no government subsidies; rather, funding comes from private foundation grants, corporate contributions, and contracts.